The Living Shakespeare

By DAVID KLEIN, Ph.D.

Professor Emeritus of English, City College of New York

Twayne Publishers, Inc.   ::   New York

TO THE MEMORY
OF THE ONLIE BEGETTER OF
THESE INSUING CHAPTERS
Mr. J. A.

A quarter of a century ago, in a time that tried men's souls, Professor Alwin Thaler asserted (*Shakespeare and Democracy*, p. 34) that "Shakespeare had many significant things to say of problems that still concern democracy today: of the causes of war, for example, and of the rise of tyrannies, of intolerance, of poverty, of the class struggle, and of public opinion." The trial is still on, and I present these pages in the same conviction. Their timeliness is further suggested in an observation by Professor Harry Levin of Harvard: "As we draw near to Shakespeare's 400th anniversary, I am convinced that he stands nearer to us than he did to his readers and spectators during most of the intervening years."

It is a pleasant duty to express my indebtedness to the late Joseph Auslander, who suggested the subject of this book, and supplied the two inspiring poems that open and close chapter 1, and with whom I was in constant consultation during the writing. It is saddening to reflect that he is not here to see the work he sponsored presented to the world.

Contents

Contents

PROEM

Tell us, Milord of Stratford and of Rhyme,
What word for us, what tidings for our time?
Stout trumpeter of all brave trumpets rung
In all the varied splendors of our tongue,
Trumpet the faith that stirred our passions when
The world was young, and we were younger men;
The strength our fathers found in simple things:
The way a lark at heaven's lintel sings
(And lifts the heavy heart on his small wings);
Proud April's clarion, the daffodil;
Dew-treading dawn . . . one star . . . a quiet hill
That points the mind to contemplation still . . .
O yet remind us what a work is man:
Not dust's quintessence, but a god who can
Order his own tremendous destiny,
In scope unfettered, in decision free
To choose 'twixt conscience and catastrophe!

JOSEPH AUSLANDER

CHAPTER 1

"The Time Is Out of Joint" Hamlet I.V. 189

WHAT SHAKESPEARE said is of compelling interest to us today because he spoke not only of things eternal, but of things that are—we trust— *not* eternal, but which do concern us today. Problems that plagued the people of his day plague us today. No date can be set upon his many vituperative reflections on the flagrant injustices inhabiting the governments of the world. They have a familiar ring. The most famous one is part of the well-known soliloquy beginning "To be or not to be":

> For who would bear the whips and scorns of time,
> The oppressor's wrong, the proud man's contumely,
> The pangs of dispriz'd love, the law's delay,
> The insolence of office, and the spurns
> That patient merit from the unworthy takes,
> When he himself might his quietus make
> With a bare bodkin?

That Hamlet's resentment represents Shakespeare's own feeling is evident from the fact that it had already been expressed in Sonnet 66:

> Tir'd with all these, for restful death I cry:
> As, to behold desert a beggar born,
> And needy nothing trimm'd in jollity,
> And purest faith unhappily forsworn,
> And gilded honour shamefully misplac'd,
> And maiden virtue rudely strumpeted,
> And right perfection wrongfully disgrac'd,
> And strength by limping sway disabled,
> And art made tongue-tied by authority,
> And folly, doctor-like, controlling skill,
> And simple truth miscall'd simplicity,
> And captive good attending captain ill.

11

These lines sound like an amplified echo, reverberating the distant voice of Koheleth:

I returned, and saw under the sun, that the race is not to the swift, nor the battle to the strong, neither yet bread to the wise, nor yet riches to men of understanding, nor yet favor to men of skill.

The same despairing outcry down through the ages.

"Art made tongue-tied by authority." Thus simply and effectively does Shakespeare register his protest against government censorship. One can only speculate what thoughts were in his mind that could not be expressed. Altogether, Shakespeare was not happy with the pettiness displayed by his fellow man, whom he credited with infinite potentiality, in the exercise of power. Isabella, in *Measure for Measure,* observes:

> Could great men thunder
> As Jove himself does, Jove would ne'er be quiet;
> For every pelting, petty officer
> Would use his heaven for thunder.
> Nothing but thunder! Merciful Heaven,
> Thou rather with thy sulphurous bolt
> Splits the unwedgeable and gnarled oak
> Than the soft myrtle; but man, proud man,
> Dress'd in a little brief authority,
> Most ignorant of what he's most assur'd,
> His glassy essence, like an angry ape,
> Plays such fantastic tricks before high heaven
> As makes the angels weep; who with our speen,
> Would all themselves laugh mortal.

Shakespeare's bitterest arraignment of human behavior issues from the mouth of King Lear, whose madness has relieved him of his inhibitions:

A man may see how this world goes without eyes . . . see how yond justice rails upon yond simple thief . . . change places, and, handy-dandy, which is the justice, which is the thief? Thou hast seen a farmer's dog bark at a beggar? . . . and the creature run from the cur? There thou mightst behold the great image of authority: a dog's obeyed in office.
Thou rascal beadle, hold thy bloody hand!
Why dost thou lash that whore? Strip thy own back;
Thou hotly lusts to use her in that kind
For which thou whip'st her . . .

Through tatter'd clothes great vices do appear;
Robes and furr'd gowns hide all. Plate sin with gold,
And the strong lance of justice hurtless breaks;
Arm it in rags, a pigmy's straw does pierce it.

The sentiment in the last four lines we summarize in the phrase,
"Money talks," and Shakespeare elsewhere expands it into

O, what a world of vile ill-favored faults
Looks handsome in three hundred pounds a year.

and again, in an unparalleled diatribe from the misanthropic lips
of Timon:

Gold! yellow, glittering, precious gold!
Thus much of this will make black white, foul fair,
Wrong right, base noble, old young, coward valiant.
Ha! you gods, why this? What this, you gods? Why, this
Will lug your priests and servants from your sides,
Pluck stout men's pillows from below their heads:
This yellow slave
Will knit and break religions; bless the accurs'd;
Make the hoar leprosy ador'd; place thieves,
And give them title, knee, and approbation,
With senators on the bench; this is it
That makes the wappen'd widow wed again;
She, whom the spital-house and ulcerous sores
Would cast the gorge at, this embalms and spices
To the April day again. Come, damned earth;
Thou common whore of mankind, I will make thee
Do thy right nature. Thou'rt quick,
But yet I'll bury thee: thou'lt go, strong thief,
When gouty keepers of thee cannot stand.

In the United States we have recently discovered the existence
of the poor. Shakespeare, long ago, felt the pathos of their existence. Never was the plight of the poverty-stricken painted in such
devastating imagery as flows from the imagination of King Lear,
who has learned what suffering is. Swaying and shivering in the
pitiless tempest into which he has been cast out by his granite-
hearted daughters, thoughts crowd in on him that had never
approached his consciousness before; and he apostrophizes:

You houseless poverty,
Poor naked wretches, wheresoe'er you are,

> That bide the pelting of this pitiless storm,
> How shall your houseless heads and unfed sides,
> Your loop'd and window'd raggedness, defend you
> From seasons such as these? O' I have ta'en
> Too little care of this! Take physic, pomp;
> Expose thyself to feel what wretches feel,
> That thou may'st shake the superflux to them,
> And show the heavens more just.

Occupation with the problem of poverty is thus declared to be a function of government. To be sure, the simple solution presented in the last four lines is hardly sound economic doctrine. Apparently, Shakespeare was preoccupied with this doctrine (with the problem he certainly was preoccupied), for he repeats it in this same play: The blinded Gloucester speaks:

> Let the superfluous and lust-dieted man,
> That slaves your ordinance, that will not see
> Because he does not feel, feel your power quickly;
> So distribution should undo excess,
> And each man have enough.

Life was a precious thing to Shakespeare—all life. We know how intoxicated he was with the products of "the bounteous housewife Nature." The life of the most insignificant creature was dear to him. Titus Andronicus notices his brother Marcus strike at something with a knife:

Titus. What dost thou strike at, Marcus, with thy knife?
Marcus. At that that I have kill'd, my lord, a fly.
Titus. Out on thee, murderer! thou kill'st at my heart:
Mine eyes are cloy'd with view of tyranny.
A deed of death done on the innocent
Becomes not Titus' brother. Get thee gone;
I see thou art not for my company.
Marcus. Alas, my lord, I have but kill'd a fly.
Titus. But! How if that fly had a father and mother?
How would he hang his slender gilded wings
And buzz lamenting doings in the air!
Poor harmless fly,
That, with his pretty buzzing melody
Came here to make us merry! and thou has kill'd him.

How, then, must he have rated a human life? The destruction of life was an abomination to him. Shakespeare treated much of war, but the motif that keeps repeating is the loss of life and the attendant human misery. His utterances on this theme would make an apt accompaniment to Frank Capra's photographs of war. In the anonymous *The Contention,* on which Shakespeare based his *Henry the Sixth,* the King announces that he will go speak with Jack Cade, the rebel leader:

> Go back to them and tell them this from me:
> I'll come and parley with their general.

That is all. Shakespeare expands this thus:

> I'll send some holy bishop to entreat,
> For God forbid so many simple souls
> Should perish by the sword! And I myself,
> Rather than bloody war shall cut them short,
> Will parley with Jack Cade, their general.

The King, in *Henry the Fifth,* seeking to learn the mood of his men regarding his war in France, mingles with them disguised as a common soldier, and engages in conversation:

Bates. He may show what outward courage he will, but I believe, as cold a night as 'tis, he could wish himself in Thames up to the neck; and so I would he were, and I by him, at all adventures, so we were quit here.

King Henry. By my troth, I will speak my conscience of the king: I think he would not wish himself any where but where he is.

Bates. Then I would he were here alone; so should he be sure to be ransomed, and a many poor men's lives saved.

York, in *Henry the Sixth,* to satisfy his personal ambition, declares:

> I will stir up in England some black storm
> Shall blow ten thousand souls to heaven or hell.

Speaking of the usurping Bolingbroke, King Richard the Second foresees that

> Ere the crown he looks for live in peace,
> Ten thousand crowns of mothers' sons
> Shall ill become the flower of England's face;
> Change the complection of her maid-pale peace
> To scarlet indignation, and bedew
> My pastures' grass with faithful English blood.

This prophecy is presently repeated and elaborated by the
Bishop of Carlisle:

> The blood of English shall manure the ground,
> And future ages groan for this foul act:
> Peace shall go sleep with Turks and infidels,
> And in this seat of peace tumultuous wars
> Shall kin with kin and kind with kind confound:
> Disorder, horror, fear, and mutiny
> Shall here inherit, and this land be call'd
> The field of Golgotha and dead men's skulls.

The fulfillment of this prophecy is the theme of Shakespeare's
King Henry the Sixth.

Henry V's answer to the Dauphin's mocking message:

> And tell the pleasant prince this mock of his
> Hath turn'd his balls to gun-stones, and his soul
> Shall stand sore charged for the wasteful vengeance
> That shall fly with them; for many a thousand widows
> Shall this his mock mock out of their dear husbands,
> Mock mothers from their sons, mock castles down;

The dying Clifford, in *Henry the Sixth*, apostrophizes the King:

> Henry, hadst thou sway'd as kings should do,
> I and 10,000 in this luckless realm
> Had left no mourning widows for our death.

The ruthlessness of the profession of war is illustrated in *Coriolanus*. Volumnia, the granite-hearted mother of the hero, proudly
boasts: "Before him he carries noise, and behind him he leaves
tears." And Coriolanus, addressing his weeping wife, says:

> Ah, my dear,
> Such eyes the widows in Corioli wear,
> And mothers that lack sons.

That is a way to console her! Henry the Fifth gives the order that
every soldier shall cut the throat of his prisoner. What an image
that presents! Shakespeare does not allow such an opportunity
for satirical comment to slip by. One of the soldiers speaks up:

The King most worthily hath caused every soldier to cut his prisoner's
throat. O, 'tis a gallant King!

It would seem that the nature of war has not changed a bit since Saul committed the unpardonable sin of sparing the life of a single Amalekite. Oliver Cromwell piously reported: "it hath pleased God to bless our endeavors at Tredan. The enemy were about 3000 strong in the town. We refused them quarter. I believe we put to the sword the whole number of the defendants. I am persuaded that this is a righteous judgment of God upon these barbarous wretches." In the course of our involvement in Korea, we were engaged in what went by the name of Operation Killer, in which the order was that no prisoners were to be taken. In the Six-Day War the Jordanian brigades that were to invade Israel received written instructions to occupy the villages and slaughter every man, woman, and child.

In *Troilus and Cressida* it is with a special relish that Shakespeare gives expression to his abhorrence of war. Thersites tells us what the war is all about:

Here is such patchery, such juggling, such knavery! All the argument is a cuckold and a whore; a good quarrel to draw emulous factions and bleed to death upon!

The august Homeric heroes are debunked, are called "waterflies, diminutives of nature"; the mighty Ajax, idol of the Athenians, is a thickheaded lout, and Achilles, the invincible Achilles, the offspring of divinity, is made out to be a dastard of dastards.

The utter senselessness of war is further emphasized in *Hamlet*. The captain in Fortinbras' army answers Hamlet's question what the war is about:

> Truly to speak, and with no addition,
> We go to gain a little patch of ground
> That hath in it no profit but the name.
> *Hamlet.* Why, then the Polack never will defend it.
> *Captain.* Yes, it is already garrison'd.

Which makes Hamlet muse:

> I see
> The imminent death of twenty thousand men,
> That for a fantasy and trick of fame
> Go to their graves like beds, fight for a plot
> Whereon the numbers cannot try the cause,
> Which is not tomb enough and continent
> To hide the slain.

Does this seem an absurd exaggeration? In the year 1968 it took an international commission to halt hostilities precipitated by the conflicting claims of India and Pakistan to the admittedly worthless Rann of Kutch, altogether some few hundred square miles in extent. Ridiculous enough—and depressing; but not as ridiculous as the trouble brewing at the time of this writing between India and Ceylon over Kachcha Tivu, an island lying in the Palk Strait between the two countries. It is one-fifth the size of New York's Central Park. The opposition parties in India have demanded that Prime Minister Indira Gandhi despatch troops and warships to the scene. Here, surely, is a "plot whereon the numbers cannot try the cause."

The full significance of Shakespeare's attitude toward war can be realized only if we view it in historical perspective. War was not looked upon as something reprehensible. Far from it. The anguished soldier Othello bids farewell to "the pride, pomp, and circumstance of glorious war;" and Mark Antony sums up the greatness of Julius Caesar in the interrogation, "Are all thy conquests, glories, triumphs, spoils, shrunk to this little measure?" The activating attitude down through the centuries is well exemplified in the man who has been extolled as the embodiment of wisdom—none other than Socrates, who, Xenophon tells us, is confident that the young man Autolicus, who has just won the prize at the Olympic games, is resolved to achieve further glory, extending the boundaries of his country. There is no thought of questioning the ethics of a war of aggression, a war for conquest. And how about the four centuries that have elapsed since Shakespeare? Even if we ignore the raving of a Treitschke, who declares: "War is elevating. What a perversion of morality to wish to abolish heroism among men!," or a Bernhardi, who avers that war "is not only a biological law but a moral obligation and, as such, an indispensable factor in civilization", we cannot escape the implication of the answer to the question, "Who are our schoolboys' heroes?" If any external influence contributed to the formation of Shakespeare's judgment on this subject it had to come from the remote past, when Isaiah saw a vision of the world wherein nation did not lift up sword against nation, neither did they learn war any more.

A more sinister origin of war than the impulse to conquest is the need to distract attention from domestic grievances. Henry the Fourth's deathbed advice to his son is: "Be it thy course to busy giddy minds with foreign quarrels." The advice is followed, as depicted in *Henry V*.

Perhaps the most graphic, and the most daring, example of Shakespeare's indictment of war is found in *Henry V*. The disguised King is chatting with his soldiers:

K. Hen. Methinks I could not die anywhere so contented as in the king's company, his cause being just and his quarrel honorable.
Williams. That's more than we know ... But if the cause be not good, the king himself hath a heavy reckoning to make; when all those legs and arms and heads, chopped off in battle, shall join together at the latter day, and cry all "We died at such a place"; some swearing, some crying for a surgeon, some upon their wives left poor behind them, some upon the debts they owe, some upon their children rawly left. I am afeard there are few die well that die in battle; for how can they charitably dispose of any thing when blood is their argument? Now, if these men do not die well, it will be a black matter for the king that led them to it.

King Henry attempts to refute Williams' argument with a string of irrelevancies. But Williams is in a strong position when he bluntly affirms, "That's more than we know," concerning the justness of the cause. Henry had decided upon the invasion of France because of his father's deathbed advice "to busy giddy minds with foreign quarrels." The last speech in *Henry IV, Part Two,* immediately following Henry's ascent to the throne, is spoken by Henry's brother, Lancaster:

> I will lay odds that, ere this year expire,
> We bear our civil swords and native fire
> As far as France. I heard a bird so sing,
> Whose music, in my thinking, pleas'd the King.

It is only after the arrival of ambassadors from France bringing the answer to Henry's demand that the throne of that realm be evacuated to make room for his ascent, that he calls on the clergy to justify and sanctify his predetermination. They not only do this, they spur him on with a vehement urgency. All practical objections are brushed aside. With a sadistic delight hardly becoming his profession, the Archbishop of Canterbury awakes remembrance of the bloody feats of the King's ancestors:

Stand for your own; unwind your bloody flag;
Look back into your mighty ancestors:
Go, my dread lord, to your great-grandsire's tomb,
From whom you claim; invoke his warlike spirit,
And your great-uncle's, Edward the Black Prince,
Who on the French ground play'd a tragedy,
Making defeat on the full power of France;
Whiles his most mighty father on a hill
Stood smiling to behold his lion's whelp
Forage in blood of French nobility.
O noble English! that could entertain
With half their forces the full pride of France,
And let another half stand laughing by,
All out of work, and cold for action.

The Archbishop is abetted by the Bishop of Ely: "With your
puissant arm renew their feats. You are their heir"—with more in
the same vein.

The church has its own reasons for encouraging Henry in his
ambition. This we learn from a conversation between the Archbishop of Canterbury and the Bishop of Ely:

Cant.   That self bill is urged,
Which in the eleventh year of the last king's reign
Was like, and had indeed against us pass'd,
But that the scambling and unquiet time
Did push it out of farther question.
Ely. But how, my lord, shall we resist it now?
Cant. It must be thought on. If it pass against us,
We lose the better half of our possession;
For all the temporal lands which men devout
By testament have given to the church
Would they strip from us. . . .
Ely. This would drink deep.
Cant.   'Twould drink the cup and all.
Ely. But what prevention?
Cant. The king is full of grace and fair regard.
Ely. And a true lover of the holy church. . . .
How now for mitigation of this bill
Urg'd by the commons?
Cant. I have made an offer to his majesty, . . .
As touching France, to give a greater sum
Than ever at one time the clergy yet
Did to his predecessors part withal.

Three and a half decades ago history repeated itself. The Church of Spain found itself in a similar situation. In the last of the five years' grace granted it by the Spanish Republic, to adjust itself to separation from the state, it took the needed step to recover its old position—and a volley was fired from the steeple of the Barcelona Cathedral. This time bribery would not have served.

Othello's magnificent lyric in glorification of the profession of war only demonstrates the greatness of Shakespeare as a dramatist. His own abhorrence of war was not allowed to interfere with his delineation of character. Othello is a soldier, and would speak like a soldier.

Joseph Auslander's fervent appeal to Shakespeare prefixed to this book cannot be dismissed as an instance of the chronic gripe of the older generation, which stubbornly clings to custom, helplessly resists change, and finds itself unable to adjust itself to a new order of things. If ever any older generation could be pardoned for murmuring it is the present one. The process of change has advanced with such dizzying rapidity that, compared with the world today, the still undue Utopia of Edward Bellamy looks like the prosiac projection of an unimaginative mind. Never before has one been penalized for traveling *slower* than forty-five miles an hour. Never before was caloric deficiency advertised as a virtue ("the fatness of these pursy times"!) Never before did we chafe under our confinement to this little globe: we have space longings in us. Never before was mankind seriously aware of being poised on the brink of total self-destruction.

A revolution of such magnitude could not but result in a radical disturbance in human relations. It is not that we have come to *disobey* the old rules. Rather, the old rules have disappeared completely. To New Yorkers, the Kitty Genovese case is the most striking example. A young woman is murdered before at least fifty sets of human eyes. Not one voice is raised, not one telephone touched. It is nobody's business. The same kind of social confusion and human disassociation can be seen in any crowded subway, where over-civilized man merges with pre-historic beast in endless undulations of shove and push. It is as if our moral sense has been paralyzed by the dizzying rate of "progress." Our language shows the same sense of utter loss. Slaughter is "pacification." Imprisonment is "re-location." Hoax is "public relations," and fraud is "image manipulation."

The reaction we are having to this dwindling of the moral sense is a violent one, and the effects far-reaching.

The world has acclimated itself to an atmosphere of permanent war. Values of beauty and truth have been divorced more decisively than ever. Right and good have surrendered to expediencey. In international relations this is nothing new: witness the recent farce played at the United Nations following the Six-Day War. No principle of conduct has received such a tongue-lashing from Shakespeare as this expediency (in Shakespeare's English it is called Commodity). When King Philip of France, for political considerations, breaks his oath to champion the cause of Prince Arthur, and joins in a league with the usurper John, the uninhibited and articulate Bastard explodes into passionate utterance:

> Mad world! mad kings! mad composition!
> That same purpose-changer, that sly devil,
> That broker, that still breaks the pate of faith,
> That daily break-vow, he that wins of all,
> Of kings, of beggars, old men, young men, maids,
> That smooth-faced gentleman, tickling Commodity.
> Commodity, the bias of the world,
> The world, that of itself is poised well,
> Made to run even upon even ground,
> Till this advantage, this vile-drawing bias,
> This sway of motion, this Commodity,
> Makes it take head from all indifferency,
> From all direction, purpose, course, intent.
> And this same bias, this Commodity,
> This bawd, this broker, this all-changing word,
> Clapp'd on the outward eye of fickle France,
> Hath drawn him from his own determin'd aid,
> From a resolv'd and honorable war,
> To a most base and vile-concluded peace.

Shades of Munich! In the anonymous play, *The Troublesome Reign of King John*, of which Shakespeare's play is a recast, the theme of the Bastard's tirade is not even suggested. It emerged from Shakespeare's contemplation of mankind.

Thomas Aquinas stated: "Truth is the last end of the entire universe, and the contemplation of truth is the chief occupation of wisdom." The present generation would understand little of what he was talking about, and would care less. In totalitarian states truth is declared to be whatever serves the state. In Schiller's *Standbild zu Zais* the pertinacious quest for truth leads to tragic consequences. Pilate asked Jesus, "What is truth?" and rushed away to escape the answer. If truth is such a mysterious and troublesome thing, why bother about it? The appearance of truth is an adequate substitute—more than adequate: it is to be preferred. A graphic illustration of the difference between the turn of the century and today: at the turn of the century a young man would proudly say: "My girl is pretty." Today he would proudly say: "My girl looks pretty." To him it's the same thing. We need Shakespeare now to open our eyes to the ugliness of the world of illusion which we have shaped to dwell in.

The employment of cosmetics is nothing new; it is older than civilization. But it was never accepted as part of the daily life of the people as a whole. In Shakespeare's day it was confined to that section of society which provided the milieu for his plots. But even there the practice was not brazenly open. It was supposed to be secret. Hamlet only hears of it: "I have heard of your paintings too. God has given you one face, and you make yourselves another." It has driven him to madness, he declares. Nevertheless, from Berowne, in *Love's Labor's Lost*, we learn that the practice was so common that naturally healthy cheeks were suspected of being painted; common enough to disgust Shakespeare, and evoke from him numerous caustic references. Apparently the prevalence of the fashion was of recent advent, for in Sonnet 68 he speaks nostalgically of the former uncorrupted days:

> Thus is his cheek the map of days outworn,
> When beauty liv'd and died as flowers do now,
> Before these bastard signs of fair were born,
> Or durst inhabit on a living brow;
> Before the golden tresses of the dead,
> The right of sepulchres, were shorn away
> To live a second life on second head;
> Ere beauty's dead fleece made another gay.

Outside the class of "our painting Gentle-women," as Earle, in his *Microcosmography*, calls them, face-painting prevailed, as one would expect, among the prostitutes. Hunting for an apt comparison, King Claudius, in *Hamlet*, states: "The harlot's cheek, beautified with plastering art, is not more ugly"; and Pompey, the pimp in *Measure for Measure*, arguing to prove his occupation to be a "mystery," that is, an honorable craft, resorts to this syllogism:

Painting, sir, as I have heard say, is a mystery; and your whores, sir, being members of my occupation, using painting, do prove my occupation to be a mystery.

In his comedy *Le Demi-Monde,* Dumas introduces this dialogue (Barrett H. Clark's translation):

> OLIVIER (*looking into the whites of her eyes*). What have you— there?
>
> VALENTINE. Where do you mean?
>
> OLIVIERS It's all black around your eyes.
>
> VALENTINE. You're just like all the others: you're going to tell me that I paint my eyebrows and lashes. When I think that fully half my friends believe that I paint—!
>
> OLIVIER. And the other half are sure!
>
> VALENTINE. The idea!
>
> OLIVIER. Don't you use powder?
>
> VALENTINE. The way every woman does—
>
> OLIVIER. And rouge?
>
> VALENTINE. Never.
>
> OLIVIER. Never?
>
> VALENTINE. Just a touch, in the evenings—sometimes.
>
> OLIVIER. And don't you touch up a little around the eyes?
>
> VALENTINE. It's the fashion.
>
> OLIVIER. Not among decent women, anyway.

That was about a hundred years ago. In our own country there are a few who still remember when a rouged face was a trade mark. If we boys caught sight of a painted face we would run ahead half a block and turn around to get a good view as the owner came up. John Masefield could then speak freely of "painted whores", without running the risk of offending the whole sex. Once the mania got started it spread with incredible rapidity, and it was not long before the experience of entering an assemblage of women was like stepping into a realm of Edgar Allan Poe's creation, peopled by beings with uncanny countenances, with lurid lips and gory claws. But one could still escape the nightmare by associating with people of education and intelligence. The campus was not part of that weird realm. But today even the faculty is infected. Today there is no interrlation between face-painting and the wearer's intellectual level. In fact, the adoration of the artificial has become one of the distinctive characteristics of the age. False eyelashes, which were once a joke, are now common dress for young women—and not women from showbusiness or the slums, but normal, refined young women, who work in offices and have husbands, and send their children to private schools. When she prepares a Saturday snack for the children, who are glued in a worldless, witless spell to the television as cartoon villains are chased by cartoon heroes, it may be a plastic bowl of French Frauds, a new product that boasts of its unreality in its name itself. Then she will wake her husband, who has been seriously considering buying a false mustache and sideburns, so he can be fashionable on the weekends. After she prepares him a breakfast of Tang and Instant Sanka she puts on her "Fabulous Fake" fur coat, which she prefers to real fur and pays more for, and hurries to the weatherproof, dome-encased shopping center where she has an 11:00 beauty shop appointment. She is thirty-two and she is having some wrinkles taken out of her face. When she grows older her visits to the beauty parlor will become more frequent, more determined. Perhaps she will be tempted by wonder drug remedies for the process of aging, such as procaine or methadrine. In the meantime, she occupies herself with tinting and re-tinting her hair and polishing her fiberglass flowers.

Of course there is nothing wrong with assisting nature. The farmer, the gardener, the physician, the surgeon, all assist nature. Supply nature with the tools and the materials that she needs for any particular job, and she will do the job, according to her own inexorable laws. The woman thinks that by dying her hair blonde she is no longer a graying woman of forty-five. Appearance becomes reality—symptomatic of the age she lives in. With all her modern sophistication she is as illogical as sweet, innocent Perdita, who in *Winter's Tale* who will not approve of any changes in nature resulting from human mediation:

> *Perdita.*   Sir, the year growing ancient,
> Not yet on summer's death, nor on the birth
> Of trembling winter, the fairest flowers o'th'season
> Are our carnations, and streak'd gillyflowers,
> Which some call Nature's bastards. Of that kind
> Our rustic garden's barren; and I care not
> To get slips of them.

Polixenes.   Wherefore, gentle maiden,
Do you neglect them?
  Perdita.   For I have heard it said
There is an art which in their piedness shares
With great creating Nature.
  Polixenes.   Say there be:
Yet Nature is made better by no mean
But Nature makes that mean; so, over that art
Which you say adds to Nature, is an art
That Nature makes. You see, sweet maid, we marry
A gentler scion to the wildest stock,
And make conceive a bark of baser kind
By bud of nobler race. This is an art
Which does mend Nature, change it rather, but
The art itself is Nature.
  Perdita.   So it is.
Polixenes. Then make your garden rich in gilliflowers,
And do not call them bastards.
  Perdita.   I'll not put
The dibble in earth to set one slip of them;
No more than were I painted I would wish
This youth should say 'twere well, and only therefore
Desire to breed by me.

Thus she admits that the carnations and gillyflowers are "the fairest flowers o'th'season," and concedes the point made by Polixenes, yet she cannot in her mind dissociate the work of the horticulturist from face-painting. To her they are both interferences with nature. The latter, which the modern girl describes as assistance to nature, is indeed interference—obstruction, in fact. The coated lips, deprived of exposure to sun and air, like the enwrapped stalk of celery, lose whatever natural color they had.

So complete has been the triumph of appearance over reality, that even the beautiful woman paints her face. If anything is more pathetic it is the now common picture of the old dowager with rainbows traversing her wrinkled face. Aside from the fact that a lie is in its very essence ugly, only the utter loss of esthetic bearings can explain what women are doing to their faces today. Pictures painted by a chimpanze can find a market; and a black-and-white daub that turns out to be the work of a twenty-two-month-old child can win a prize at an art exhibit near Los

Angeles. According to the newspaper report one of the judges describes the drawing as "expressionistic" and "beautifully designed and exciting."

In the passage from *Hamlet* quoted above. King Claudius presents the harlot's painted cheek as the acme of the ugly. It is little exaggeration to compare the perimeter of the woman's open mouth to that on the face of the circus clown. It is the distinction of the human countenance to possess individuality; for each human being possesses individuality which that countenance reveals. A thousand cows look alike: is is a rare thing for two human beings to look alike. Painting the face destroys the diversity, and makes for a dead conformity—especially the treatment of the mouth, which is the most mobile, the most sensitive, part of the face, the most revelatory of individual character, its lines so subtle that it is the despair of the portrait painter. God has given them one face and they make themselves another, following the fashion. "Ay, fashion you may call it." Look what women are doing with their eyes today. One used to see such eyes in the slums of a Sunday morning when the husband had come home late the night before in a questionable shape. But the women then were not inclined to show them off. Tastes have changed.

The reader must have noticed that Shakespeare's Sonnet 68, quoted previously, is addressed to a man. In Shakespeare's day rouging was not confined to the weaker sex. In *Much Ado about Nothing* the friends of Bendick tease him for doing it—a sure sign that he is in love. Today, men use bronzing and tanning creams, in or out of love. Also, they approve of the use of make-up in women (sixty years ago they were violently against it), thus unconsciously betraying the male's traditional downgrading of womankind.

The extent of the triumph of Appearance over Reality in our daily life is further illustrated by the institution known as Public Relations. Its functionaries are expert at painting Images. For a fee they will paint and expose any image of you that will serve your purpose: and the image need have no resemblance to the original. The recent "The Selling of the President: 1968" brilliantly dissects the multi-tentacled public relations organization that convinced America to elect Richard Nixon. A subsidiary institution goes by the fitting name of Ghost Writer. The images we worship are presented to us as writers and thinkers. Knowledge of the identity of the ghost doesn't make any difference to us: we carelessly allow the credit to the image, and "his" utterances will be quoted by posterity. If, as Shakespeare avers, "Truth is truth to th'end of reckoning," this cannot be regarded as a healthy state of affairs.

Is there a remedy? Can Shakespeare, whom Professor Schelling described as "the greatest of human minds," come to our assistance? Macbeth despairingly turns to the doctor for help:

> If thou couldst, doctor, cast
> The water of my land, find her disease,
> And purge it to a sound and pristine health,
> I would applaud thee to the very echo,
> That should aplaud again.

The doctor makes no reply; for he had already answered him:

> Therein the patient
> Must minister to himself.

Macbeth does not really expect an answer, and he does not stay for one. He knew what his land's disease was. It was of his own implanting, and his remorseful soul would have rejoiced to be able to apply the remedy. It would have razed out the written troubles of his brain, and cleansed his stuffed bosom of that perilous stuff which weighed upon his heart. But it was too late. We too can be ministered to only by ourselves. But we must first become aware that we are sick. If we "cast the water of our land," we shall find that our disease is the decaying of our ideals.

Half a century ago, if you found yourself in a European railroad compartment with a group of natives, almost inevitably the subject of American materialism would be broached. It was useless for you to suggest that to America's material success there was joined a considerable degree of traditional idealism. You would point to our passionate interest in free education (there was little of that in Europe, none at all above the lower grades), to our free public libraries (there were none in Europe outside of England, and very few there), our museums, our sold-out theaters and concert halls. You would get hot under the collar, while your opponent would mumble along with the exacerbating imperturbability of perfect knowledge. He has never been to America, but he didn't have to go to that inconvenience to know

all about it. It may come to one with a little shock of surprise
how few European intellectuals have ever thought it worthwhile
to cross the ocean to visit us.

I happened to be in the waiting-room of the new railway station in Geneva, a city renowned as a center of culture, just when
the finishing touches were being put on. My eye was attracted to
a strange notice on the wall, neatly pencilled, ready for the painter's brush. It read: "Ol travelers wil not be cold wen trens liv."
A little deciphering enabled me to read: "All travelers will not be
called when trains leave." But for the accident of my being on the
spot at the time, the gibberish would have been fixed (not permanently, one hopes) on the wall of the imposing newly erected
structure—a symbol of European complacency. Apparently it did
not occur to the perpetrator that his own knowledge of the English language could possibly be deficient. Try to imagine a boo-
boo like that committed in America!

To show that the intervening years have not disturbed that
complacency in this respect, I shall select two examples from
Nino Lo Bello's recent experiences—reported in the Miami *Herald*
—one for the tragic consequences possible, the other for its blunt
brevity. Number one: On a Russian ship the following instructions for the use of the life-preserver were posted on the cabin
door:

"Helpsavering apparata in emergings behold many whistles! Associate
the stringing apparata about the bosoms and meet behind. Flee then
to the indifferent lifesaving shippen obediencing the instructs of
the vessel chef."

Number two: Notice on the elevator door of a Roumanian hotel
lobby:

"The lift is being fixed for the next days. During that time we regret
that you will be unbearable."

I once got into a conversation on shipboard with a Dutch
clergyman who was returning from a three-week stay in America.
Of course that made him an authority. His opinion of our nation
was what I expected; only he couched it in vocabulary befitting
a clergyman: "America is not interested in the unseen." Specify-
ing, he pointed out that we had not produced a Shakespeare or a
Milton. That much I conceded, but argued that we were still a

young nation; and I gently pressed the point that we had nevertheless done something in that direction. We had produced—
here I began to enumerate—a Longfellow, a—"Longfellow!" he interrupted, "Is he an American?" And I was not displeased to learn
that his opinion of Longfellow was even loftier than mine. This is
only one of numerous instances of the same kind that I could
cite, illustrating the smug ignorance abroad regarding America.
But it will suffice.

It is with a feeling of chagrin that I must admit that today I
could not rise to the defense with the same fervor. It cannot be
denied that the spiritual values that distinguished us have de-
clined. Our intellectual life has gravely deteriorated, its symbols
brought into mild contempt. Scholars feel self-conscious about
making use of their academic degrees. One of them, twitted in
company for "showing off" his Phi Beta key, snapped back, significantly, "I want to prove that I'm not ashamed of it." We joke
about "egg-heads" and "pointy-heads," and ridicule the notion of
a "brain-trust" influencing national policy. We used to encourage
higher education and research. Today they are discouraged.
Formerly a student registering for the doctorate would pay one
moderate fee, and be entitled to take as many courses as he
pleased, and to take as long as he needed. Today each course has
a price. Even the principle of free education is being under-
mined, as notably illustrated by what happened in the State of
New York. As far back as 1847 the city of New York, by popular
vote, affirmed the revolutionary principle that the common man
has an equal right with the privileged to a higher education: it
created The Free Academy (the name later changed to The City
College) with the mandatory provision embodied in its character
that there be no charge for tuition. In the course of time other
municipal colleges and a number of State colleges were established, as the need arose. From their portals has issued intellectual and political leadership for a democratic nation.

For well over a century, tampering with the mandatory free-
tuition provision was unthinkable. Then came a multimillionaire
Governor who, employing the political devices at his command,
succeeded in having it eliminated, and a fee imposed upon the
State colleges. The municipal colleges are still free, but they
dwell under a threatening shadow. A delegation of students that
appeared before the legislature to protest against the elimination

was greeted by the Governor's legislative spokesman with the
scornful question: "Who do these kids think they are?"

Our whole educational system is in a parlous state. With this
plaint our ears are pelted on every side. The responsibility for the
deplorable situation must rest squarely on the shoulders of the new
"science" of education. This "science" was discovered about the
beginning of the century, and immediately books upon books,
dutifully written by members of school boards, began to crowd
the school bookshelf—packed with balderdash. Anybody with
open eyes could see what the result would be. A beloved teacher
of mine at City College of New York, Professor Adolph Werner,
one of the few truly great men it has been my privilege to associate with, wrote to me as far back as 1911: "I sometimes regret
that I had to do some subjects and not others, and that some were
presented in the way in which they were and not in another; but
I rejoice every day that my schooling was of the old, unreformed,
unimproved style. I am awfully sorry for the *heute heranwach-
sende Jugend.*" His misgivings have been more than confirmed.
One is prompted to subscribe to an opinion expressed by a writer
in *Harper's Magazine* some twenty years ago. He closed a series
of articles with the declaration that if some college president
were moved to give his institution a real lift, his first step should
be to fire the Professor of Education.

Perhaps one reason why the scholar is not eager to display his
academic credentials is that they have been cheapened. A student can obtain the bachelor's degree, and higher degrees, by
majoring in home-making, or salesmanship. One university found
it convenient to make use of its prospectus to inform applicants
that it does not give courses in embalming. In short, our educational system is predominantly geared to preparing students, not
for living, but for *a* living. Today the good clergyman's complacent affirmation could not be so vehemently protested. At this
writing a great institution of learning, in a locality where the
intellectual life has been a tradition, publishes this announcement: "The College's pioneering division of Adult Education will
be discontinued at the close of the current semester." The reason
given: "increased demand for vocational and technical subjects
as opposed to 'cultural courses.'" Not on the "unseen," but on the
very visible symbols of physical satisfaction, our eyes are focused.
The accumulation of these has been the aim of our striving, and

success has attended our efforts. We call the achievement prosperity. Against "the fatness of these pursy times" Shakespeare issues a word of warning. Hamlet meditates on Fortinbras' senseless military expedition:

> This is he imposthume of much wealth and peace,
> That inward breaks, and shows no cause without
> Why the man dies.

Any objection to the applicability of Hamlet's diagnosis to our case on the ground that there has been no peace, may be dismissed. The unremitting war of the last half century has not touched our shores. It has wrought destruction in other lands, but to our United States it has brought prosperity. Indeed, the sudden cessation of conflict could here be a frightening thought. The profit-making horror-show in Vietnam is, of course, a case in point.

The nature of our ailment is similarly explained by the Archbishop of York in *Henry IV*:

> . . . we are all diseas'd,
> And with our surfeiting and wanton hours
> Have brought ourselves into a burning fever.
> And we must bleed for it.

Both of the extracts quoted carry a warning of dire consequences. Shakespeare further directs us to learn a lesson from history:

> There is a history in all men's lives
> Figuring the nature of the times deceas'd;
> The which observ'd, a man may prophesy,
> With a near aim, of the main chance of things
> As yet not come to life, which in their seeds
> And weak beginnings lie intreasured.
> Such things become the hatch and brood of time.

What does history teach us that is relevant to our present situation? Not in poetry, which may be discounted, but in sober prose, Gibbon reports briefly: "The decline of Rome was the natural and inevitable effect of immoderate greatness. Prosperity ripened the principle of decay." Could anything be more apropos? Our resemblance to ancient Rome is startling. Microcosmically the state of our union is revealed in the report on our theater for 1965, in *Time* magazine: "Broadway continued to be beset by urban blight. Part of what was wrong was the audience itself—too old, too prosperous, too complacent to be bothered about the basics of the human dilemma." Are we then doomed? If we are what Shakespeare says we are, the answer is no:

What a piece of work is a man! how noble in reason! how infinite in faculty! in form and moving how express and admirable! in apprehension how like a god! the beauty of the world, the paragon of animals!

If that is what we are, then when we go wrong it must be because we have not made use of our infinite faculty. "What is a man?" Hamlet asks, harping on the same thought.

> If his chief good and market of his time
> Be but to sleep and feed? a beast, no more.
> Sure He that made us with such large discourse,
> Looking before and after, gave us not
> That capability and god-like reason
> To fust in us unused.

Pernicious are the consequences of mental inertia. "O, then we bring forth weeds/When our quick minds lie still," exclaims the conscience-smitten Antony.

The remedy, then, is apparent: education. We must learn how to use our tremendous powers. "Folly and ignorance," Shakespeare tells us, are "the common curse of mankind"; and again: "Ignorance is the curse of God, Knowledge the wing wherewith we fly to heaven." This conception of education as a wing to carry us toward the infinite, tallies with the view maintained by the great Scottish scholar, philosopher, and teacher, Thomas Davidson, known as "the last of the Humanists," who defined education as "conscious evolution." What a vista this thought opens up to us! Nature attained the acme of her evolutionary operation with the emergence of man—a sadly imperfect creature, but of infinite potentiality. Where Nature left off, man must take hold and carry on. Thus the further evolution of the human species will be determined by the system of education adopted. If it is geared to a higher standard of living, as it has been for some time, we may be lifted to Mars, but we will never be winged to heaven. A higher standard of living? How much higher a standard do we want? Three cars instead of two in every garage? Not a higher standard of *living*, but a higher standard of *being*, must deter-

mine the direction of our conscious evolution. We must educate
for leisure, not for labor. What we glorify in the civilization of
the Periclean age was the product of leisure. Can we keep our
eyes shut to the fact that the age of automation is already upon
us, and is creating disturbing problems for us? The Greeks had
slaves to provide the material precondition for their civilization.
We have automation. Its coming brings us face to face with
Aristotle's proposition (to him self-evident, to us challenging)
that the noble employment of leisure is the highest aim which
man can pursue, that states that have not been prepared for this
must fall. This is the proud challenge with which human ingenu-
ity has confronted us—a challenge from which there is no escape.

Man will at last be in a position to apply unhampered the
divine faculties with which he is endowed. Obviously it is for
that kind of liberated man that our educational program must be
devised. This will involve a revolutionary break with custom.
Shakespeare warns us that a break with custom may be found to
be imperative. That is one of the facts about which he is most
emphatic:

> What custom wills in all things should we do't.
> The dust on antique time would lie unswept,
> And mountainous error be too highly heapt
> For truth to o'erpeer.

How wonderfully this is put!

If we do not sell our birthright for a mess of pottage, permitting our "capability and godlike reason to fust in us unus'd,"
another quadricentennial of Shakespeare's birth will be cele-
brated by a superior race, having a high degree of intelligence
(our level of intelligence has been scientifically measured by
"Madison Avenue"; its findings are reflected in the commercials)
and a lofty moral concern; a race which rigidly distinguishes between truth and appearance, and regulates its life accordingly;
a race that has outgrown prejudice; a race so highly developed
that it is capable of being the master, instead of the victim, of
material prosperity, and does not require the impetus of suffering
to be ennobled; a race from whose composition the primordial
savage instincts have been extirpated; a race that long since had
fulfilled the ancient prophecy that "nation shall not lift up sword

against nation, neither shall they learn war any more"; a race that
will justify Shakespeare's final vision:

> O wonder!
> How many goodly creatures are there here!
> How beauteous mankind is! O brave new world
> That has such people in it!

If, however, above the din of the marketplace we do not heed
"the ominous stern whisper from the Delphic cave within," it
may well be that when that day arrives, an untenanted and sterile
earth will be spinning through space to all eternity. "But yet the
pity of it!"—Moses, Homer, Socrates, Michelangelo, Shakespeare,
Bach, Einstein—in the short hour of man's strutting and fretting
upon this stage!—"O the pity of it!" We might have been on the
threshold; instead we are on the brink.

In this hour of trial a word of cheer from our wise mentor,
William Shakespeare, is indeed welcome:

> Before the curing of a strong disease,
> Even in the instant of repair and health,
> The fit is strongest; evils that take leave,
> On their departure most of all show evil.

In other words, "The nearer the dawn the darker the night,"
as Longfellow rendered this bit of folk wisdom. A devout prayer
for the realization of this hope from the lips of Joseph Auslander,
whose appeal to Shakespeare opened this volume, will bring this
chapter to a close:

> Now, when our hearts are troubled and we stare
> Up at an ominous and iron sky,
> Striving to read the riddle written there,
> Asking the heavens whither, the hills why;
> Now, when the air we breathe is thick with hate,
> And malice and confusion hedge us round,
> And by a single hair the fearful weight
> Of human destiny is faintly bound—
> O send us leaders, Lord, serene and whole,
> Anchored in truth, though ringed about with lies,
> The courage of the prophets in their soul,
> The candor of the children in their eyes. . . .
>
> Let us have done with wrangling, Lord, and crawling:
> **Give us the faith to keep the sky from falling.**

CHAPTER 2

Shakespeare and The Common Man

A VOWED CHAMPIONS of the proletariat have not found Shakespeare friendly to the common man. To him, they point out, in their limited knowledge, the common man was, at best, a nameless "First Citizen," "Second Citizen," "Third Citizen," (unaware that Shakespeare also introduces us to "First Gentleman," "Second Gentleman," "Third Gentleman," and even to "First Lord," "Second Lord," "Third Lord"); at worst, he was a many-headed beast. These critics have deliberately placarded themselves, and donned blinders which confine their vision to a narrow horizon. Their opinion may therefore be disregarded in a serious discussion of the question. But they find authority in so distinguished a writer of many books as George Brandes.

Brandes speaks of "the passionate disdain for the masses possessing Shakespeare's soul," and devotes pages to variations on the theme:

Thus much can be declared with absolute certainty, that the anti-democratic spirit and passion of the play [*Coriolanus*] sprang from no momentary political situation, but from Shakespeare's heart of hearts . . . For the people he felt nothing but scorn . . . On reading her [Volumnia's] speeches we realize the satisfaction and relief it was to Shakespeare to vent himself in furious invectives, through the medium of his dramatic creations.

He even derives from Shakespeare's hatred of the people an explanation for his indifference to the publication of his plays:

He had watched the growth of narrow-minded prejudice, had seen the triumphant progress of that pious stupidity which condemned his art as a wile of the devil; and his detestation of the mass of men, past, present, and to come, made him equally indifferent to their praise, or blame. Therefore it pleased him to express this indifference through the medium of Coriolanus.

Quite a heap of misanthropy to saddle one man with! Brandes admits his awareness that his views will not find favor in certain quarters; but—here follows the classic example of self-appraisal— "It is enough for us if our perception is fine and keen enough to recognize him in his works, and we must actually put on blinders not to see on which side Shakespeare's sympathies lie here." It simply does not penetrate his consciousness that possibly *he* is the one who has put on the blinders. He speaks of "the time when Shakespeare's dramas were interpreted by liberal professors, who involuntarily brought them into harmony with their own ideas," and presently comes out with the rash pronouncement that "some few on this earth are men, the rest are *spawn,* as Menenius calls them." It was *he,* then, who involuntarily brought Shakespeare's dramas into harmony with his own ideas: it was *he* who had put on the blinders. Hence Brandes's verdict, too, may be set aside with that of the radical propagandists.

We cannot, however, act so summarily in the case of sober students of Shakespeare such as Professor Albert H. Tolman and Professor Alwin Thaler when they express similar views. Tolman affirms that *"Julius Caesar* and *Coriolanus* seem to show with special clearness Shakespeare's hostility to the common folk," and Thaler, referring to Hazlitt, says: "It is small wonder that he was out of patience with Shakespeare for loading the dice against the people—as Shakespeare, the contemner of mobs, undeniably did in *Coriolanus."* To be sure, these utterances are only concessions, relative to these two plays: the tenor of the treatment of the subject by both these scholars is a defense of Shakespeare against charges such as those leveled against him by Brandes. Says Thaler: Upon turning from Shakespeare's impassioned fulminations against the plebeian mob of Rome to the more calmly considered studies of his own English kings, nobles, and commoners, I think we shall find that *Coriolanus* is, after all the exception that proves the rule.

But there is a decisive quality about those utterances that must give us pause. In *Coriolanus* (forgetting *Julius Caesar* for the moment) Shakespeare does *not* show hostility to the common folk, and he does *not* load the dice against the people. How could scholars of such standing go so far wrong?

The answer to the question will be found in the passage just quoted. Thaler speaks of "Shakespeare's impassioned fulminations against the plebeian mob of Rome," when he should say

"Coriolanus's impassioned fulminations." Both Tolman and Thaler have fallen into the common error of identifying the playwright with the character he has created. Such identification might pass with lesser dramatists; but Shakespeare was the great playwright he was because he knew how to give his characters their own life. They consequently made the additional mistake of seeing the people of Rome through the eyes of the character whom they identified with Shakespeare.

There is no mob in *Coriolanus*. There is a perplexed populace caught in an unhappy dilemma. The great mistake it makes is hazarding its own interest in its commendable eagerness to show appreciation of desert. Coriolanus has deserved well of his country. He has earned the right to be honored with the consulship. But he is an enemy of the people, a patrician with a fanatic hatred of the plebeians. Once he wielded consular power there would be an end to the rights of the commoners. That is a foregone conclusion. One of the tribunes, who represent the people, states the case aptly: "Then our office may, during his power, go sleep."

To be elected consul the candidate had to have the approval of the commoners. Custom demanded that he appear before them dressed in a "gown of humility," show them his wounds, and ask them for their votes. In the play people gather to debate the matter, and we hear this discussion:

First Citizen. Once if he do require our voices, we ought not to deny him.
Second Citizen. We may, sir, if we will.
Third Citizen. We have power in ourselves to do it, but it is a power that we have no power to do; for if he show us his wounds and tell us his deeds, we are to put our tongues into those wounds and speak for them. Ingratitude is monstrous, and for the multitude to be ungrateful were to make a monster of the multitude; of the which we being members, should bring ourselves to be monstrous members.
First Citizen. He himself stuck not to call us the many-headed multitude.
Third Citizen. We have been called so of many; not that our heads are some brown, some black, some auburn, some bald, but that our wits are so diversely colored: and truly, I think if all our wits were to issue out of one skull, they would fly east, west, north, south, and their consent of one direct way should be at once to all the points o' the compass.

Second Citizen. Think you so? Which way do you judge my wit fly?

Third Citizen. Nay, your wit will not so soon out as another man's will: 'tis strongly wedged up in a blockhead. Are you all resolved to give your voices? But that's no matter; the greater part carries it. I say, if he would incline to the people, there was never a worthier man.

Does this sound like a mob? Is it customary for a mob to indulge in self-analysis? Yet these are the people whom Walt Whitman called "The stupid canaille that Coriolanus cannot stomach."

Coriolanus appears before them. They give him their votes, wistfully begging him to be good to them after he gets into power. He addresses them in searing sarcasm, which does not sink in until the ceremony is over:

Second Citizen. To my poor unworthy notice, he mock'd us when he begg'd our voices.

Third Citizen. Certainly he flouted us downright.

First Citizen. No, 'tis his kind of speech: he did not mock us.

Second Citizen. Not one amongst us, save yourself, but says he used us scornfully. He should have show'd us his marks of merit, wounds received for 's country.

Third Citizen. He said he had wounds, which he could show in private; and with his hat, thus waving it in scorn, "I would be consul," says he: "aged custom, but by your voices, will not so permit me; your voices, therefore." When we granted that, here was "I thank you for your voices: thank you: your most sweet voices: now you have left your voices, I have no further with you." Was not this mockery?

Then comes the realization that it is not too late: "He's not confirm'd: we may deny him yet." And they do deny him: not in turmoil, but in organized fashion, disciplined and directed by the tribunes, their representatives.

There is, indeed, little excuse for finding in this play justification for attributing to Shakespeare a hostile attitude toward the common people. In the very first scene the audience, or, certainly, the reader, is put on his guard against such an unwarranted impeachment. The famished people are on the brink of an uprising. Any moment now may come the explosion. At such a time one would expect riot, mad tumult, to prevail. Not at all! There is debate; there is soul-searching; there are divided counsels. One impetuous citizen, a direct-actionist, wants to begin by killing Coriolanus, "chief enemy to the people." He is interrupted by another citizen: "One word, good citizens." To which the other retorts: "We are accounted *poor* citizens, the patricians good. What authority surfeits on would relieve us: if they would yield us but the superfluity, while it were wholesome, we might guess they relieved us humanely; but they think we are too dear. The leanness that afflicts us, the object of our misery, is as an inventory to particularize their abundance; our sufferance is a gain to them." The patricians, he goes on, "suffer us to famish, and their storehouses crammed with grain; make edicts for usury, to support usurers; repeal daily any wholesome act established against the rich, and provide more piercing statutes daily to chain up and restrain the poor. If the wars eat us not up, they will." How strangely familiar some of this sounds! Thus Shakespeare supplies justification for their cause. The speaker ends his harangue with the protest, "The gods know I speak this in hunger for bread, not in thirst for revenge." The other citizen demands: "Would you proceed especially against Caius Marcius?" "Against him first: he's a very dog to the commonalty." "Consider you what services he has done for his country?" "Very well; and could be content to give him good report for't but that he pays himself by being proud." "Nay, but speak not maliciously." "I say unto you, what he hath done famously, he did it to that end: though soft-conscienced men may be content to say it was for his country, he did it to please his mother, and to be partly proud; which he is, even to the altitude of his virtue."

This is a correct appraisal of the man, as borne out by events. Yet these are the people whom Coriolanus cannot forgive for having the audacity to hold any opinion regarding what is going on in the world:

> Hang 'em! They say!
> They'll sit by the fire, and presume to know
> What's done in the Capitol; who's like to rise,
> Who thrives and who declines; side factions, and give out
> Conjectural marriages; making parties strong,
> And feebling such as stand not in their liking,
> Below their cobbled shoes.

He thus lets us know how active was their civic consciousness.

When the soldiers he leads at the assault on Corioli are forced back to their trenches, Coriolanus has a splendid opportunity to vent his sulfuric hatred:

> All the contagion of the south light on you,
> You shame of Rome! you herd of—Boils and plagues
> Plaster you o'er, that you may be abhorr'd
> Further than seen, and one infect another
> Against the wind a mile!

Here, too, Shakespeare is careful to save us from slipping into the error of siding with Coriolanus. A short distance away Cominius has led a similar assault, and been similarly forced to retreat. How does he address his soldiers (drawn from the same population)?

> Breathe you, my friends, well fought; we are come off
> Like Romans, neither foolish in our stands,
> Nor cowardly in retire.

This episode is introduced, of course, to set off, by contrast, the character of Coriolanus. There is no other reason for the duplication. The way Coriolanus, at any time, behaves toward his soldiers, needs have no relation to the demands of the existing situation. It is chronic and predictable. In her imagination, Volumnia, his mother, proudly follows him to the battlefield; she is addressing her daughter-in-law:

> Methinks I hear hither your husband's drum;
> See him pluck Aufidius down by the hair;
> As children from a bear, the Volsces shunning him:
> Methinks I see him stamp thus, and call thus:
> "Come on, you cowards! you were got in fear,
> Though you were borne in Rome."

We see that he does not let her down. That is the way he was, and the way his mother had brought him up to be. Earlier in the play he had already characteristically expressed himself on the reliability of the people from whom his army was drawn:

> He that trusts to you,
> Where he should find you lions, finds you hares;
> Where foxes, geese: you are no surer, no,
> Than is the coal of fire upon the ice,
> Or hailstone in the sun.

The irony here becomes obvious. *He* is the one not to be depended on. When things do not go his way, he turns traitor, goes over to the enemy, and wages war against his own country; thus confirming the opinion expressed by the citizen that he performed his titanic acts out of pride in achievement, not out of loyalty to his country.

If Shakespeare did not depict the plebeians as a rabble, he did not, at the same time, advance them as representatives of a superior type. Their perceptions are limited, like those of most people, at any level of the social scale. For instance, they look upon Menenius as their friend: "Worthy Menenius Agrippa," they declare, "one that has always loved the people." The fact is that he despises the people—despises them as heartily as does Coriolanus. He is the familiar type of politician who knows how to cajole himself into the people's confidence. When Volumnia urges her son to promise the people that if he is elected he will do his best to be their friend, even if he doesn't mean it, Menenius chimes in:

> This but done,
> Even as she speaks, why, their hearts were yours;
> For they have pardons, being ask'd, as free
> As words to little purpose.

He is experienced with words to little purpose. So thoroughly has he succeeded in ingratiating himself with the masses that he can afford to take chances on calling them rats to their faces. Yet Professor Tolman can say: "So far as the play of *Coriolanus* contains a wise, impartial chorus-master, whose opinions we may accept as those of the poet himself, it is the humorous old patrician Menenius Agrippa ... He is the character in the play with whom we can most fully sympathize." How can a genuine scholar go so far wrong? again I ask. Some of Shakespeare's plays must be read many times before preconceptions are wedged out, leaving the poet's intention visible.

The way you feel about Brutus and Sicinius, the tribunes, the official representatives of the plebeians, will depend on which side you stand, or rather, on which side you think Shakespeare stands, in the conflict between Coriolanus and the people. If you are not on the side of the people you will look upon them through the eyes of Menenius, who is most articulate in down-grading them. That is how Tolman sees them: "It is certainly the tribunes Brutus and Sicinius whom the poet scorns most of all. They are artful demagogues of the most unworthy type." If you think that Shakespeare is on the people's side, you will adjudge them well-meaning officials, conscientiously active in the performance of their appointed functions. To be sure, they are politicians, who try to make certain that they get the credit that is due, or partly due, them. But there is nothing dishonest about that, nothing to brand them as belonging to "the most unworthy" type. They are not afraid to stand up to the enemy of the people, and with dignity. When Coriolanus scornfully says to Brutus, "By yond clouds, let me deserve so ill of you, and make me your fellow tribune," Sicinius responds:

> You show too much of that
> For which the people stir. If you will pass
> To where you are bound, you must inquire your way,
> Which you are out of, with a gentler spirit,
> Or never be so noble as a consul,
> Nor yoke with him for tribune . . .
> You speak o' the people
> As if you were a god to punish, not
> A man of their infirmity.

Before Coriolanus is through he realizes that they are right: "I melt, and am not of stronger earth than others."

When the tribunes order the banishment of Coriolanus they know that they are taking a risk. After all, he is an impregnable bulwark against an enemy. Like statesmen, however, they decide upon the lesser of two evils: "To eject him hence but our danger, and to keep him here our certain death;" that is, the death of democratic participation in the government. That Coriolanus would turn traitor and lead a foreign army against Rome does not enter their heads. The report that he has actually done that they consider absurd. When the report is confirmed they wisely turn to Menenius to intercede. He calls Coriolanus "my son," and who, Coriolanus admits, loved him "above the measure of a father." When he bitterly berates them for what they have done they avoid recrimination, and calmly enter their plea:

> *Sicinius.* Nay, pray, be patient: if you refuse your aid
> In this so never-needed help, yet do not
> Upbraid's with our distress. But, sure, if you
> Would be your country's pleader, your good tongue
> Might stop our countryman.
> *Brutus.* Only make trial what your love can do
> For Rome, towards Marcius.

Menenius. Well, and say that Marcius
Return me, as Cominius is return'd,
Unhead; what then?
    Sicinius. Yet your good will
Must have that thanks for Rome, after the measure
As you intended well.

These are the speeches of statesmen; these are not the speeches
of "artful demagogues of the most unworthy type." Statesmanlike
too is the tribune's reply in the following dialogue:

Menenius. Be that you seem, truly your country's friend,
And temperately proceed to what you would
Thus violently redress.
    Brutus. Sir, those cold ways,
That seem like prudent helps, are very poisonous
Where the disease is violent.

The truth of Brutus's statement was brought home to the world
not many years ago, and current events prove that the lesson has
not yet been mastered.

Menenius is irked when told that the tribunes are "reverend
grave men," and the worst thing that he can say of them is that
they, in their capacity as magistrates, are too painstaking in ad-
judicating what to him, the patrician, are trivial cases: "You wear
out a good wholesome forenoon in hearing a cause between an
orange-wife and a forset seller," whereas he is "said to be something imperfect in favoring the first complaint"; that is, in dis-
posing of a case after hearing only one side. They can answer to
the purpose: "Come, come, you are well understood to be a per-
fecter giber for the table than a necessary bencher in the Capitol."

In two significant respects Shakespeare departs from his source.
In Plutarch Coriolanus requests the liberation of a formerly rich
well-descended friend of his in the captured city of Corioli, and
the request is presumed granted. In Shakespeare the episode is
thus presented:

Coriolanus. I sometime lay here in Corioli
At a poor man's house; he used me kindly:
He cried to me. I saw him prisoner; . . . I request you
To give my poor host his freedom.
    Lartius. Marcius, his name?
    Coriolanus. By Jupiter! forgot.

And the matter is pursued no further. He was willing to show his gratitude; but the man was, after all, only "a poor man." Noble as his instincts were, Coriolanus's horizon could not reach beyond the periphery of the aristocracy.

In Plutarch we read that "there were great troubles and commotions at Rome" after the banishment of Coriolanus. In Shakespeare a halcyon spell seems to hover over the city of Rome:

> *Sicinius.* We hear not of him, neither need we fear him;
> His remedies are tame i' the present peace
> And quietness of the people, which before
> Were in wild hurry. Here do we make his friends
> Blush that the world goes well, who rather had,
> Though they themselves did suffer by't, behold
> Dissentious numbers pestering streets, than see
> Our tradesmen singing in their shops, and going
> About their functions friendly.
> *Brutus.* We stood to't in good time. Is this Menenius?
> *Sicinius.* 'Tis he, 'tis he: O, he is grown most kind of late.
> *Both Tribunes.* Hail sir!
> *Menenius.* Hail to you both!
> *Sicinius.* Your Coriolanus
> Is not much miss'd, but with friends:
> The commonwealth doth stand, and so would do
> Were he more angry at it.
> *Menenius.* All's well.

When, at the beginning of the play, news is brought that the Volsces are in arms against Rome, Coriolanus's comment is: "I am glad on't: then we shall ha' means to vent our musty superfluity," the musty superfluity being the common people. In the scene just quoted, deliberately created, Shakespeare reveals to us that in the world as it ought to be—and can be—it is the Coriolanus type that constitutes the superfluity.

At one point in the play we are startled to hear Coriolanus, of all people, lashing out upon the principle of conservatism. The speech is quoted on page (29). Nowhere else has the urgency for social change been so eloquently argued. Isolated from the text, it would strike one as the utterance of an advanced twentieth century liberal, a man with social vision. We are not faced here with an inconsistency. Shakespeare only highlights Coriolanus's blindness to himself, and accentuates his utter lack of social vision. The social change which he so vigorously advocates involves a return to the old aristocratic order, unrestricted.

Coriolanus represents a universal phenomenon. We find his counterparts among those administering the affairs of mankind today. They tell us much about a "changing world," and the necessity for adjustment to it; however, any change adversely affecting respective interests is stubbornly resisted.

We see no mob in *Coriolanus*, but we do in *Henry the Sixth* and in *Julius Caesar*. In each case the mob acts like a mob. How else would the objectors expect the mob to act? Or would they deny Shakespeare the privilege of depicting a mob at all? Are the masses so sacred a cow to them that they must be treated only with sentimental tenderness? The mobs in Dickens behave no less irrationally than do those in Shakespeare, yet who would accuse Dickens of hostility to the common man? In *Julius Caesar* the people are driven insane under the skilful manipulation of a master spellbinder, so they behave like madmen. Let him, whoever he be, whatever his station, who knows himself to be impervious to the assaults and blandishments of the spellbinder, cast the first stone. The most colossal, and the most successful of all recorded spellbinders is popularly known by the name of Madison Avenue. The target for its battery is selected from no particular segment of society. The world is its oyster, and it has the sword to crack it open. There is no essential difference between the response it attracts and that accorded a demagogue. The Roman populace in the play has been condemned for being so easily swayed from one side to another. Brutus's oration is, unconsciously, pure demagoguery, proving nothing; yet I have known teachers of English who found it convincing. Then what is to be expected of the untutored? Without accepting Brandes's contemptuous dictum that "some few on this earth are men, the rest are spawn," I am afraid it cannot be denied that we are one vast mob, susceptible of being swayed this way and that. "All are the multitude," declares Ben Jonson, "only they differ in clothes, not in judgment or understanding."

In *Henry the Sixth* Shakespeare assigns to the commons the responsibility of forcing the king to speak and act, for once, as if he were every inch a king. We heard Coriolanus sneer at the commons for presuming "to know what's done in the Capitol." In *Henry the Sixth* the commons do know what's done in the capitol. The court swarms with hostile nobles, led by the queen's paramour, the Duke of Suffolk, and the young king feels himself helpless. The commons decide that "it were but necessary" that he "were waked." Accordingly, through the Earl of Salsbury, they send a message—and an ultimatum—to the king:

> Dread lord, the commons sends you word by me,
> Unless false Suffolk straight be done to death,
> Or banished fair England's territories,
> They will by violence tear him from your palace
> And torture him with grievous lingering death.

A novel kind of lynching party this! The king yields, Suffolk is banished, and for the first time, and for the moment, we have a modicum of respect for Henry.

Later in the play these same commoners are up in rebellion, goaded by the Pretender Jack Cade. Only the diligent reader will discover that Shakespeare has taken the trouble to provide an explanation for the crazy uprising. The good King Henry, the saintly King Henry, casually and unconcernedly gives his emissary instructions how to raise the funds to cover the expenses of transporting his contracted bride from France:

> For your expenses and sufficient charge,
> Among the people gather up a tenth.

Thus unobtrusively, without affirming any casual relation, Shakespeare lets us perceive, if we are interested, the unhealthy condition that perforce fostered the rebellion, turning the rational populace introduced earlier into a wild and ridiculous mob. Technically the passage is quite dispensable. Nothing that goes before, or comes after, is visibly dependent on it. Nobody is interested in the question. The audience has not, even remotely, given it a thought. Yet Shakespeare introduces it. It is in such lines that Shakespeare admits the deserving into his private confidence.

The play affords another example of the same category. The location is Saint Albans, that boasts a shrine. A miracle is announced, and a man is brought in before the royal presence who declares he has just received his eyesight at the shrine, having been born blind. To the accompaniment of much fun the fraud is exposed, and the liar and his wife are sent off to be whipped. The scene has absolutely no connection with the rest of the play. It cannot even be defended as a desirable comic interlude in serious matter, like the drunken porter scene in *Macbeth*, for such has already been included in the preceding scene. One wonders why it was lugged in, till the eye catches a short line muttered by the wife as the couple is hustled out: "We did it for pure need;" and one is tempted to conclude that Shakespeare wrote the whole scene for the sake of that one line, to illustrate the causal connection between poverty and crime. Thus Shakespeare anticipates the product of Jim Casey's cogitation: "An' I begin to see then. It's need that makes all the trouble."

Those who hold that in his views and attitudes Shakespeare was an aristocrat point triumphantly to the following passage in *Winter's Tale*:

> This is the prettiest low-born lass that ever
> Ran on the green-sward. Nothing she does or seems
> But smacks of something greater than herself,
> Too noble for this place.

The lines are spoken by Polixenes, king of Bohemia, about Perdita, the lost daughter of Leontes, king of Sicilia, brought up from infancy by a shepherd. This is Tolman's comment: "Is there not something of courtier-like servility in this extreme glorification of kingly blood?" How else would one expect King Polixenes to think and speak? It cannot be too strongly emphasized, and emphasized again, that Shakespeare was a playwright, and believed that the purpose of playing "was and is to hold, as 'twere, the mirror up to nature." He could not have been the great dramatic artist he was if he had not been able to present sympathetically views and attitudes foreign, or even repugnant, to himself. When he wrote a play he was not interested in soothing anybody's sensibilities, certainly not those of ten centuries beyond. His creations must be true to themselves. His king must think and speak like a king. If he does not, then we are justified in assuming that he is the mouthpiece for Shakespeare's thoughts. That is the case with the French king in *All's Well That Ends Well*. In that play Count Bertram is scandalized at the thought of marrying Helena, a physician's daughter, recommended to him by the king:

> A poor physician's daughter my wife! Disdain
> Rather corrupt me ever!

Thereupon the king treats him to a long lecture:

> 'Tis only title thou disdain'st in her, the which
> I can build up. Strange is it that our bloods,
> Of color, weight, and heat, pour'd all together,
> Would quite confound distinction, yet stand off
> In differences so mighty. If she be
> All that is virtuous, save what thou dislik'st,
> A poor physician's daughter, thou dislik'st
> Of virtue for the name. But do not so.
> From lowest place when virtuous things proceed,
> The place is dignified by the doer's deed.
> Where additions swell's, and virtue none,
> It is a dropsied honor. Good alone
> Is good without a name. Vileness is so.
> The property by what it is should go,
> Not by the title . . . Honors thrive
> When rather from our acts we them derive
> Than our foregoers. The mere word's a slave
> Debauch'd on every tomb, on every grave
> A lying trophy, and as oft is dumb
> Where dust and damn'd oblivion is the tomb
> Of honor'd bones indeed. What should be said?
> If thou canst like this creature as a maid,
> I can create the rest. Virtue and she
> Is her own dower; honor and wealth from me.

No feudal king could entertain such ideas. This is Shakespeare talking. In fact, in the source for the play, Paynter's version of a tale in the *Decameron,* "the Kyng was very lothe to graunte hym unto her." What other explanation can there be for Shakespeare's departing from his original, and in the process doing violence to probability, than that he sought an opportunity to say things that he thought should be said?

It is worth noting that the speech is in rhyme, hence belonging to Shakespeare's earliest period, being part of the unrevised version of the play, as it was produced in 1589 under the title *Love's Labor's Won.* It thus represents Shakespeare's thinking when he was a young man of twenty-five.

What Shakespeare really thought of royalty we can gather, not from the words uttered by Polixenes, but rather from the gusto with which he directs the procession of that sorry lot of kings and would-be kings and dukes and earls who throng through the

pages of his histories. Regarding the significance of these pla
for us today, Professor Thaler calls our attention to the fact th
in his old age, Walt Whitman, the poet of American democra
intimated "that in the future, Shakespeare may be remember
in America primarily because he exposes most powerfully t
evils of the old order, the 'necessity' for the new order, which
still the American way" and he quotes:

Will it not be strange if the author of "Othello" and "Hamlet" is d
tin'd to live in America, in a generation or two, less as the cunni
draughtsman of the passions, and more as putting on record the fi
full exposé—and by far the most vivid one, immeasurably ahead
doctrinaires and economists—of the political theory and results .
which America has come on earth to abnegate and replace?

This utterance marks a radical conversion in Whitman's thinkir
Earlier he had declared that Shakespeare "is not only the a
of feudalism, but incarnated, uncompromising feudalism, in]
erature . . . the democratic requirements are insulted on eve
page." Whitman only illustrates the necessity of frequent ar
intensive reading if one seeks to learn Shakespeare's messag
Without it, as we have seen, there is bound to be dogmatic utte
ance of doubtful validity. An additional example worth noting
the following decisive conclusion arrived at by M. M. Reese (T
Cease of Majesty, p. 320): ". . . it is quite evident that Shak
speare approves of him [Henry]; just as, in his own drama
terms, he approves of Isabella and does not approve of Shyloc
One might discover that Shakespeare had reservations regardi
the quality of Isabella's virtue and of Shylock's wickedness; ar
in an exhaustive article in The Fortnightly Review for 1902 A.
Bradley demonstrates that Henry V. did not have Shakespear
approval. The same is done, and done effectively, by Profess
Allan Gilbert in Patriotism and Satire in Henry V.[1]

The process of Whitman's conversion could very well ha
been initiated by a speech like the following swimming into]
ken:

> Think'st thou that I will leave my kingly throne
> Wherein my grandsire and my father sat?
> No: first shall war unpeople this my realm.

[1]In Studies in Shakespeare, Arthur D. Matthews and Clark M. Emery, e
University of Miami Press. 1953.

he shocking words are uttered by none other than the saintly
onarch Henry the Sixth, who had been so unhappy over the
uel havoc that war wreaked among the helpless masses. Shake-
*eare's intention could not but become manifest. From there
'hitman could have gone on and recalled the devastating depic-
on of royalty in *Richard II*, in imagery that reminded him of
s fellow American, Edgar Allan Poe:

> Within the hollow crown
> That rounds the mortal temples of a king
> Keeps Death his court; and there he sits,
> Scoffing his state, and grinning at his pomp.

Impressed, too, he must have been by Henry the Fifth's frank
cognition of himself, when he is disguised as a common soldier:

> :hink the king is but a man, as I am; the violent smells to him as it
> th to me; the element shows to him as it doth to me; all his senses
> ve but human conditions: his ceremonies laid by, in his nakedness
> appears but a man;

hich would recall Perdita's indignant retort following King
lixenes' brutal verbal assault upon her in *Winter's Tale*:

> I was not much afraid; for once or twice
> I was about to speak, and tell him plainly
> The self-same sun that shines upon his court
> Hides not his visage from our cottage, but
> Looks on alike.

One of the most irresponsible judgments pronounced upon
akespeare was uttered by the propagandist Ernest Crosby, who
und in Shakespeare no instance of "serious and estimable be-
vior on the part of the individuals representing the lower
isses." One must wonder how many plays of Shakespeare he
d read. Thoroughness of investigation is not within the code of
opaganda. The greatest of propagandists, Tolstoy, based his
inion of Richard Wagner on a portion of one act of *Siegfried*.
id Crosby ever read *King Lear*? Into that tempestuous, soul-
attering tragedy Shakespeare introduces a few "representing
e lower classes," to save the world from despair. The Duke of
rnwall is engaged in gouging out the eyes of the Earl of Glou-
ster, when a servant interposes. I quote the text:

First Servant. Hold your hand, my lord!
I have serv'd you ever since I was a child,
But better service have I never done you
Than now to bid you hold.
   Regan. How now, you dog!
   First Servant. If you did wear a beard upon your chin,
I'd shake it on this quarrel. What do you mean?
   Cornwall. My villain!
   First Servant. Nay, then, come on, and take the chance of anger.
   Regan. Give me thy sword. A peasant stand up thus!

The servant wounds Cornwall fatally, but is stabbed in the back
by Regan. When the wounded Cornwall is carried out, two servants remaining behind hold a memorable dialogue:

Second Servant. I'll never care what wickedness I do,
If this man come to good.
   Third Servant. If she live long,
And in the end meet the old course of death,
Women will all turn monsters.
   Second Servant. Let's follow the old earl, and get the Bedlam
To lead him where he would.
   Third Servant. Go thou: I'll fetch some flax and whites of eggs
To apply to his bleeding face. Now, Heaven help him!

Of course Shakespeare does not permit either of the royal fiends
to "come to good," or "meet the old course of death." Later an old
tenant of the Earl of Gloucester begs to be allowed to lead his
blinded master to Dover. Gloucester refuses, for fear lest the man
suffer at the hands of the duke and his wife, but he agrees to be
guided by Mad Tom, the disguised Edgar, for whom he asks the
old man to bring some covering for his nakedness. The reply of
the old man is: "I'll bring him the best 'parel that I have, come
on't what will." Thus the goodness of the human heart in a
wicked world is shown to have a dwelling-place among those
whom Crosby designates "the lower classes."

Perhaps an even more pertinent instance is afforded by *Richard
the Second,* but if Mr. Crosby shows such ignorance of *King Lear,*
he cannot be expected to have read a comparatively little known
play like this one. Richard has allowed himself to be misled by
court favorites into criminal mismanagement of the government,
with the result that he is deposed by Bolingbroke, who has a
number of those favorites executed. The matter is being dis-

cussed by the Queen's gardener and his servant. They compare
the care of the garden to the administration of the government:

> *Servant.* Why should we in the compass of a pale
> Keep law and form and due proportion,
> Showing, as in a model, our firm estate,
> When our sea-walled garden, the whole land,
> Is full of weeds; her fairest flowers chok'd up,
> Her fruit-trees all unprun'd, her hedges ruin'd,
> Her knots disorder'd, and her wholesome herbs
> Swarming with caterpillars?
> *Gardener.* Hold thy peace.
> He that hath suffer'd this disorder'd spring
> Hath now himself met with the fall of leaf.
> The weeds which his broad-spreading leaves did shelter,
> That seem'd in eating him to hold him up,
> Are pluck'd up root and all by Bolingbroke;
> I mean the Earl of Wiltshire, Bushy, Green.
> *Servant.* What, are they dead?
> *Gardener.* They are; and Bolingbroke
> Hath seiz'd the wasteful King. O, what pity is it
> That he had not so trimm'd and dress'd his land
> As we this garden! We at time of year
> Do wound the bark, the skin of our fruit-trees,
> Lest, being over-proud in sap and blood,
> With too much riches it confound itself;
> Had he done so to great and growing men,
> They might have liv'd to bear and he to taste
> Their fruits of duty. Superfluous branches
> We lop away, that bearing boughs may live;
> Had he done so, himself had borne the crown,
> Which waste and idle hours hath quite thrown down.
> *Servant.* What, think you the King shall be depos'd?
> *Gardener.* Depress'd he is already, and depos'd
> 'Tis doubt he will be.

The Queen has overheard the dialogue and steps forward.

> Why dost thou say King Richard is depos'd?
> Dar'st thou, thou little better thing than earth,
> Divine his downfall? . . .
> Pray God the plants thou graft'st may never grow.

To the Queen they are "little better thing than earth." These
men talk like wise councilors. Presumably Mr. Crosby would ac-

cept the Queen's opinion of the common man (it coincides wi
Coriolanus's) as Shakespeare's.

Crosby is also unhappy about the way Prospero, in *The Ter
pest,* speaks of Caliban:

Prospero. We'll visit Caliban my slave, who never
Yields us kind answer.
Miranda. 'Tis a villain, sir,
I do not love to look on.
Prospero. But, as 'tis,
We cannot miss him. He does make our fire,
Fetch in our wood, and serve in offices
That profit us.

To Crosby this speech is an insult to the workingman. Might v
not, with equal justice, find Shakespeare's intent in it to be a
arraignment of Prospero? To begin with, the way Prospero a
dresses Caliban is not calculated to evoke kind answer. Furthe
more, we are to judge Caliban, not by what Prospero says of hir
but by what he himself says and does. Observe the imagery th
informs his primitive mind:

I prithee, let me bring thee where crabs grow;
And I with my long nails will dig thee pig-nuts,
Show thee a jay's nest, and instruct thee how
To snare the nimble marmoset. I'll bring thee
To clust'ring filberts, and sometimes I'll get thee
Young scamels from the rock.

. . . .

Pray you, treat softly, that the blind mole may not
Hear a foot fall . . .

As wicked dew as e'er my mother brush'd
With raven's feather from unwholesome fen
Drop on you both!

He is the child of nature. Even the offense which irrevocably lo
him Prospero's favor was committed only in obedience to th
natural law. Having lived solitary he was in no position to kno
that there was a clash between the demands of nature and th
convenience of the social organization. He is the *unspoiled* chi
of nature. Shakespeare sets him off against the drunken pai
Stephano and Trinculo, whose sense of relative values has bee
distorted by civilizing influences. They abandon the execution

at to them is an act of momentous consequence, to take ad-
ntage of an opportunity to disport in the luxury of fine apparel.
liban tries to bring them to their senses:

Caliban. Let it alone, thou fool; it is but trash.
Trinculo. O, ho monster! we know what belongs to a frippery.
King Stephano!
Stephano. Put down that gown, Trinculo; by this hand, I'll have
t gown.
Caliban. The dropsy drown this fool! what do you mean
dote thus on such luggage? Let 't alone . . .
Trinculo. Monster, come, put some lime upon your fingers, and
y with the rest.
Caliban. I will have none on't. We shall lose our time.

t his words are wasted. He had mistaken them for celestial
ngs; now his eyes are opened to their shabby character:

> What a thrice-double ass
> Was I to take this drunkard for a god
> And worship this dull fool!

kespeare leaves no room here for doubt as to which he con-
red the superior.

From Caliban we learn the history of his relations with Pros-
o:

> This island's mine, by Sycorax my mother,
> Which thou takest from me. When thou camest first,
> Thou strok'dst me, and madest much of me, wouldst give me
> Water with berries in't, and teach me how
> To name the bigger light, and how the less,
> That burn by day and night, and then I lov'd thee,
> And show'd thee all the qualities o'the'isle,
> The fresh springs, brine-pits, barren place and fertile.

s was established the pattern of colonialism which has served
e or less successfully down to our generation: pet the native,
n enslave him. It should not be difficult to find a pretext:

Prospero. Thou most lying slave,
om stripes may move, not kindness! I have us'd thee,
h as thou art, with human care, and lodg'd thee
nine own cell, till thou did'st seek to violate
honor of my child.

With the self-deception that accompanies self-righteousness, Prospero first calls Caliban a "most lying slave," when the latter tells him the unwelcome truth, and then proceeds to stress his own beneficence:

> Abhorred slave,
> Which any print of goodness wilt not take,
> Being capable of all ill! I pitied thee,
> Took pains to make thee speak, taught thee each hour
> One thing or other. When thou didst not, savage,
> Know thine own meaning, but wouldst gabble like
> A thing most brutish, I endow'd thy purposes
> With words that made them known. But thy vile race,
> Though thou didst learn, had that in't which good natures
> Could not abide to be with; therefore wast thou
> Deservedly confin'd into this rock,
> Who hadst deserv'd more than a prison.

To Prospero, the supreme product of civilization, no punishment was severe enough for the mere attempt to violate the social law. Obviously, his characterization of Caliban does not tally with the truth. Before Prospero cast him out he did take a "print of goodness, and was eager to show his gratitude" ("Then I lov'd thee," etc.) and Prospero concedes that he was a docile pupil. When Stephano declares, "I was the man i' the moon when time was," Caliban eagerly responds: "I have seen thee in her, and I do adore thee: my mistress show'd me thee, and thy dog, and thy bush." The picture suggested is that of a cordial and customary teacher-pupil relationship. His acquisition of language comes in handy now. It makes him articulate in his grief over the robbery of his domain. And how choice is his imprecatory vocabularly:

> You taught me language; and my profit on't
> Is, I know how to curse. The red plague rid you . . .
>   All the charms
> Of Sycorax, toads, beetles, bats, light on you!
> For I am all the subjects that you have,
> Which first was mine own king; and here you sty me
> In this hard rock, whiles you keep from me
> The rest o' th' island.

The Tempest was written during the feverish era of discovery, exploration, and colonization. We are not surprised to see that

Shakespeare's prophetic soul was alert to the human implications involved.

On page (4) I quoted a speech of King Lear's which rightly should be repeated in this connection. It marks the moment of Lear's regeneration. He now realizes that "unaccommodated man is no more but a poor, bare, forked animal." He is no longer the pampered monarch, but "a poor, infirm, weak, and despis'd old man," one with a suffering humanity. Robert Burns used the passage to preface his poem entitled "A Winter Night." He says no more in his ninety-six lines than Shakespeare does in six—much less indeed. After reading these lines Brandes, instead of speaking of "the passionate disdain for the masses possessing Shakespeare's soul," should have spoken of the passionate *commiseration* for the masses possessing Shakespeare's soul. Noteworthy it is that in the age of assertive democracy Burns could do no better than turn to Shakespeare.

All this, and more, can be cited and has been cited to disprove the charge that Shakespeare lacked sympathy with the common man. For myself, if I sought to know how Shakespeare felt about the common man, I should not think it necessary to look into the plays for the answer, for a play is an objective portrayal, nor into his sonnets, for the sonnet was a conventional exercise; I should expect to find the answer in his lyrics, for the lyric is an outpouring of the heart. I should find the answer in the song beginning "When icicles hang by the wall." Here it is:

> When icicles hang by the wall,
>   And Dick the shepherd blows his nail;
> And Tom bears logs into the hall,
>   And milk comes frozen home in pail;
> When blood is nipp'd, and ways be foul,
> Then nightly sings the staring owl,
> Tu-whit to-who:
>   A merry note,
>   While greasy Joan doth keel the pot.
>
> When all aloud the wind doth blow,
>   And coughing drowns the parson's saw;
> And birds sit brooding in the snow,
>   And Marian's nose looks red and raw;
> When roasted crabs hiss in the bowl,
> Then nightly sings the staring owl,

> Tu-whit to who:
> A merry note,
> While greasy Joan doth keel the pot.

What a flood of fresh air breezes through these exquisite lin
They do not speak of courts and kings and battlefields. Th
speak familiarly and lovingly of happiness in the humble hon

CHAPTER 3

Four Types of Political Leader

I. JULIUS CAESAR

H. G. WELLS goes to some length to debunk the superman image of Julius Caesar that has been bequeathed to us. In his view, Caesar was merely one in a procession of dictatorially minded adventurers, each with a mercenary army behind him, who successively eliminated one another. In the first century B.C. Rome was a republic in which the few lived in lavish luxury, the many in dire distress. The rich were getting richer, the poor poorer—a set-up that sounds strangely familiar to the student of world affairs today. It was an unhealthy situation which then, as now, nurtured the germ of revolution. The masses were ready to welcome any change that held out any promise of amelioration. Caesar forged to the front by eliminating Pompey, and as a practical politician he knew how to install himself in Pompey's place as the popular idol.

Apparently Shakespeare anticipated Wells' opinion of Caesar. His references to him show that he was aware that "that Caesar was a famous man." They stress his military achievements. But these, it seems, in Shakespeare's mind were not evidence of greatness of character. The portrait of him in the play to which he applies the title is anything but a flattering one. It presents us with a pompous, superstitious, even cowardly, braggart. Already, in *As You Like It,* Shakespeare had pointed his finger at "Caesar's thrasonical brag of 'I came, saw, and overcame.'" On his first appearance in the play that bears his name, Caesar opens the scene with a single word of command, "Calpurnia!" In this way the keynote to his character is struck. As we go along we cannot help noticing that he is the first to speak in every situation in which he appears—an interesting device by which Shakespeare succeeds in stressing his egoism. The same end is served by having him objectify himself and speak of himself as "Caesar," avoiding the first person pronoun. The supersititious man is revealed in his command to Calpurnia to stand in the way of Mark Antony when he runs his ceremonial course, so that he may touch her and thus cure her of her sterility; the pompous man, in his final command: "Set on; and leave no ceremony out." Incidentally, his position as dictator is suggested to us in Mark Antony's response when told not to forget to touch Calpurnia: "When Caesar says 'Do this,' it is performed." Thus an authentic preliminary sketch of the man is presented at the beginning: as the play proceeds the sketch is rounded out into a three-dimensional portrait.

Upon the return of the procession from the "ceremonies," Brutus, who, with Cassius, has remained away, is prompted to observe:

> But, look you, Cassius,
> The angry spot doth glow on Caesar's brow,
> And all the rest look like a chidden train:
> Calpurnia's cheek is pale, and Cicero
> Looks with such ferret and such fiery eyes
> As we have seen him in the Capitol,
> Being crossed in conference by some senators.

The cynical Casca's explanation for this agitated situation is too precious, in his own words, to be paraphrased:

I can as well be hanged as tell the manner of it: it was mere foolery; I did not mark it. I saw Mark Antony offer him a crown; . . . and, as I told you, he put it by once; but, for all that, to my thinking, he would fain have had it. Then he offered it to him again; then he put it by again; but, to my thinking, he was very loath to lay his fingers off it. And he offered it the third time; he put it the third time by; and still as he refused it, the rabblement shouted, and clapped their chapped hands and threw up their sweaty night-caps, and uttered such a deal of stinking breath because Caesar refused the crown, that it had almost choked Caesar; for he swounded and fell down at it. And for mine own part, I durst not laugh, for fear of opening my lips and receiving the bad air. . . .

Brutus. What said he when he came unto himself?

Casca. Marry, before he fell down, when he perceived the common herd were glad he refused the crown, he plucked me ope his doublet and offered them his throat to cut. An I had been a man of any occupation, if I would not have taken him at a word, I would I might go to hell among the rogues. And so he fell. When he came to himself again, he said, if he had said or done anything amiss, he desired their worships to think it was his infirmity. Three or four wenches, where I stood, cried "Alas! good soul," and forgave him with all their hearts; but there's no heed to be taken of them: if Caesar had stabbed their mothers, they would have done no less.

How much information Shakespeare has packed into this surly speech! The suspicion is confirmed that Caesar aimed at the crown, thus toppling the Roman republic, and restoring the ancient monarchy. How the aristocracy reacted is indicated in Cassius' words previously addressed to Brutus:

> O! you and I have heard our fathers say,
> There was a Brutus once that would have brook'd
> The eternal devil to keep his state in Rome,
> As easily as a king.

But we also learn that Brutus' misgivings, expressed in the words, "I do fear the people choose Caesar for their king," are unfounded. The "people," too, had inherited Roman traditions, and the thought of a king in Rome was as odious to them as to the aristocracy. They were willing to accept a dictator, but not a king. Indeed, it was the aristocratic Senate that had appointed Caesar Dictator. Recent European history provides the parallel of the parliamentary body of a great nation, that had struggled desperately for nearly a century to keep its republican form alive after scuttling its monarchy, finally being reduced to the necessity of granting its executive dictatorial powers, in the hope of allaying an explosive situation. The unexpected hysterical applause with which the multitude greeted Caesar's repeated refusal of the crown brought on a fit of epilepsy, spoiled the holiday, and turned Caesar's followers into a "chidden train." Not only does Casca's graphic account give us to understand the attitude of the aristocrats toward the "rabblement," but also how they felt regarding Caesar: "An I had been a man of any occupation, if I would not have taken him at a word [i.e., to cut his throat], I would I might go to hell among the rogues." We also learn of Cicero's expressed position, which later cost him his life, and which explains why he looked "with such ferret and such fiery eyes" when he returned from the celebration.

At the same time we are told that the angry spot did glow on **Caesar's brow**. That was the mood he was in when his eye fell

on Cassius. At that sight, following his recent experience with t
crown, his vexation found expression. He calls Mark Antony:

> Let me have men about me that are fat;
> Sleek-headed men and such as sleep a-nights.
> Yond Cassius has a lean and hungry look;
> He thinks too much: such men are dangerous.
> ... But I fear him not:
> Yet if my name were liable to fear,
> I do not know the man I should avoid
> So soon as that spare Cassius. He reads much;
> He is a great observer, and he looks
> Quite through the deeds of men ...
> I rather tell thee what is to be fear'd
> Than what I fear, for always I am Caesar.
> Come on my right hand, for this ear is deaf.

Plainly, Caesar would have profited by the admonition. "Jud
not that ye be not judged." Most of us think well of men wl
read much and think much and we are apt to admire those wl
have the power to penetrate below the surface of things, benea
the deeds of men, to their motives. Evidently, Caesar had reas
to fear such men.

The last line, referring to Caesar's deafness, might sound irre
elant and superfluous. Shakespeare put it there to add to tl
accumulation of deficiences which Cassius advances to dispara;
Caesar and, at the same time, to cast a satirical glance at tl
brag preceding.

One cannot help being impressed by the number of tim
Caesar finds it necessary to disclaim all fear. The gentleman do
protest too much, methinks. We find him persisting in the san
protest the next time we meet him. The question there is wheth
Caesar will leave the house that day. It is the Ides of Marc
against which Caesar had been warned and strange supernatur
phenomena had manifested themselves during the night. Tl
question had been raised at a meeting of the conspirators ;
Brutus' house to plan the assassination. Cassius reminded h
companions:

> But it is doubtful yet
> Whether Caesar will come forth today or no;
> For he is superstitious grown of late.

:ius confidently disposes of his fears; he knows how to handle
:sar:

> I can o'ersway him; for he loves to hear
> That unicorns may be betray'd with trees,
> And bears with glasses, elephants with holes,
> Lions with toils, and men with flatterers;
> But when I tell him he hates flatterers,
> He says he does, being then most flattered.
> Let me work;
> For I can give his humor the true bent,
> And I will bring him to the Capitol.

d he makes his way directly to Caesar's house. But before he
s there, there is a scene between Caesar and his wife, Cal-
nia. She has had a bad dream about her husband and has
rd about the supernatural appearances in the city. She there-
e objects to his going out. We know that he is not indifferent
he portents, for he sends a servant to the augurers to perform
immediate sacrifice, and bring him their opinion of the result.
t toward his wife's plea he is adamant and pours out a torrent
intolerable bombast:

> Caesar shall forth: the things that threaten'd me
> Ne'er look'd but upon my back; when they shall see
> The face of Caesar, they are vanished. . . .
> . . . danger knows full well
> That Caesar is more dangerous than he:
> We are two lions litter'd in one day,
> And I the elder and more terrible;
> And Caesar shall go forth.

Calpurnia understands her husband and knows that it is only
natter of face-saving with him, so she provides an excuse:

> Alas! my lord,
> Your wisdom is consumed in confidence.
> Do not go forth today: call it my fear
> That keeps you in the house, and not your own.

ving got started, she quickly thinks of a second excuse, per-
)s a better one:

> We'll send Mark Antony to the senate-house,
> And he shall say you are not well today.

He agrees:

> Mark Antony shall say I am not well;
> And, for thy humor, I will stay at home.

Thus, while Calpurnia's appeal was merely a wifely appeal he was unyielding, but now that she has suggested a plausible excuse, he promptly consents—and says he does it for her sake.

At this point Decius enters. His arrival demands an alteration in the procedure. Instead of Caesar sending a messenger to report to the Senate, the Senate comes to him. He must now stand upon his dignity and authority. He greets Decius:

> You are come in very happy time
> To bear my greeting to the senators,
> And tell them that I will not come today:
> Cannot is false, and that I dare not, falser;
> I will not come today: tell them so, Decius.

Why this stubborn denial of what he had not been accused of? Calpurnia, disturbed at her husband's betraying himself, tries to come to his assistance: "Say he is sick," which evokes a furious exclamation:

> Shall Caesar send a lie!
> Have I in conquest stretch'd mine arm so far
> To be afeard to tell greybeards the truth?
> Decius, go tell them Caesar will not come.

What righteous indignation! Only a moment ago he was perfectly willing to send that lie. The shrewd Decius, of course, takes in the situation:

> Most mighty Caesar, let me know some cause,
> Lest I be laugh'd at when I tell them so.

Caesar condescends to describe Calpurnia's dream. Decius cleverly reinterprets the dream in such a way as to flatter Caesar's vanity. Decius pushes his advantage by announcing that the Senate has decided to crown Caesar this day, and Caesar agrees to go. At this point the conspirators arrive.

Caesar has suddenly become a changed man. The good news has put him into high spirits. Thus far we have seen only the dictator. We are now allowed to get a glimpse of the human being. His haughty and unnatural manner is suspended and he acts the cordial host. This is good drama. The planned assassination ceases to be a cut and dried, foregone affair. Our interest is renewed. We cannot help according some sympathy to the victim who so warmly welcomes, collectively and individually, the men who have come to lead him to the slaughter. However, no sooner has he taken his seat in the Senate, than he is back to the arrogant dictator and the daggers of the assassins cut him short in the midst of a torrent of braggadocio.

Thus ended the "mighty Caesar." We may express amazement, with Cassius, that

> A man of such a feeble temper should
> So get the start of the majestic world,
> And bear the palm alone.

But it did happen, and will happen again when circumstances so determine. We, in our time, have had the opportunity to watch a "sawdust Caesar," similarly created, strut and fret upon the stage a score of years, and then come to the same end as the man whose successor he considered himself to be.

2. MARK ANTONY

Caesar is dead; long live Caesar! Caesar was dead, but not the spirit of Caesar. That is the lesson his assassins were destined to learn. So long as the conditions that produced Caesar remained unchanged, his spirit would remain alive, ready for reincarnation. Perhaps Brutus learned the lesson right after the assassination. When he had finished his speech proving to the people what a noble deed he had performed for their sake, a shout came from the crowd, "Let him be Caesar!" How must he have felt when he heard that shout! After killing his best friend to rid them of a Caesar, he learns that a Caesar is what they wanted. Sure enough, no sooner had Caesar's body crumpled at the base of Pompey's statue, than his spirit found reincarnation in Caesar's second in command at the defeat of Pompey, Mark Antony.

The Antony that Shakespeare places before us in *Julius Caesar* had greatness thrust upon him. In the early part of the play we know him only as a playboy, who "revels long a-nights." Only Cassius perceives his latent possibilities. Caesar is disturbed by the fact that Cassius "looks quite through the deeds of men." But that gift is not a general possession. When, on the eve of the assassination, Cassius expresses his misgivings regarding Antony, Brutus waves him off contemptuously:

> Alas! good Cassius, do not think of him:
> If he love Caesar, all that he can do
> Is to himself, take thought and die for Caesar:
> And that were much he should; for he is given
> To sports, to wildness, and much company.

What impresses Caesar when he speaks of Antony's revelling long a-nights, is that he "is notwithstanding up," ready for the business of the day. When the call comes, he is ready. When the greatness is thrust upon him he receives it squarely on his shoulders, and promptly turns into a mature and cunning politician.

From the innocent Brutus he slyly wins permission to speak at Caesar's funeral. The audience he faces is a hostile one. It has just been convinced by Brutus, whom they worship, that Caesar had deserved to die. They have no desire to hear any other speaker, and refrain from dispersing only because Brutus urgently exhorts them to remain and listen to Antony. They remain, but the din and uproar characteristic of an excited mob persists. Antony finds himself called upon, now or never, to prove his capacity for political leadership—and he proves it triumphantly. He knows there is one word that has the magic power to arrest the attention of any in that crowd whose ears it reaches—the name of Brutus. He shouts with all the power of his lungs: "For Brutus' sake I am beholding unto you." As expected, there is a stir in the crowd: they are not sure what they heard. "What does he say of Brutus? What does he say of Brutus?" they ask one another. The answer allays the rising apprehension. "T'were best he speak no harm of Brutus here," expresses the ominous sentiment. He makes a second start, an ingratiating one: "You gentle Romans" and three more, each after a pause to allow the fringe of his audience to widen, assuring them that he has not come to praise Caesar, the thing they object to, but only to bury him. Why praise him? "The *evil* that men do lives after them," not the good. "The good is oft interred with their bones." Which, of course, is commonly the reverse of the truth. But Antony understands the mob. He knows that a mob will not stop to scrutinize a generalization.

He is now ready to proceed with the first division of his carefully planned oration. Reiterating Brutus' charge that Caesar was ambitious, he accompanies each repetition with evidence to the contrary, all the while protesting that Brutus is an honorable man. The word "honorable" is repeated so often that the irony must eventually be perceived. Now comes the emotional appeal. The occasion is a funeral—a time for mourning:

You all did love him once, not without cause;
What cause witholds you then to mourn for him?

He sets them an example. He is overcome. He cannot proceed.

My heart is in the coffin there with Caesar,
And I must pause till it come back to me.

The pause, of course, is to give him an opportunity to gauge the impression he has made. The crowd talk things over:

First Citizen. Me thinks there is much reason in his sayings.
Second Citizen. If thou consider rightly of the matter, Caesar has had great wrong.
Third Citizen.   Has he, masters?
I fear there will a worse come in his place.
Fourth Citizen. Mark'd ye his words? He would not take the crown;
Therefore 'tis certain he was not ambitious.
First Citizen. If it be found so, some will dear abide it.

All this while Antony has let tears trickle down his cheeks.

Second Citizen. Poor soul; his eyes are red as fire with weeping.
Third Citizen. There's not a nobler man in Rome than Antony.

Antony now knows that the people are with him. He has them in his hand and can play with them as he will. He had prophesied over the body of Caesar that

Domestic fury and fierce civil strife
Shall cumber all the parts of Italy . . .
And Caesar's spirit, ranging for revenge, . . .
Shall in these confines with a monarch's voice
Cry "Havoc!" and let slip the dogs of war.

It is toward the fulfilment of that prophecy that he must direct their emotions. He starts setting fire to their imagination. He takes out a document and holds it up, exposing the seal of Caesar. It is Caesar's will, he tells them. If they only knew the contents of

that document, what would they not do! They would kiss dead
Caesar's wounds; they would beg a hair off his head and be-
queath it unto their issue as a rich legacy. But he will not read it.
Oh no! He is afraid to think what they, not being wood, or stone,
might do if they knew that they are Caesar's heirs. Of course, the
clamor increases, and he reluctantly yields:

> You will compel me then to read the will?
> Then make a ring about the corpse of Caesar,
> And let me show you him that made the will.

They make a ring about the body of Caesar—and promptly forget
about the will. Does he show them "him that made the will?" Not
at all. He is not yet ready for that. Their fury must be built up in
stages to a more ferocious pitch. Instead, he shows them the
mantle covering Caesar, and they promptly forget about Caesar.
He paints a vivid picture of the assassination, pointing to the
dagger holes and identifying the perpetrator of each as if it had
a label attached. He must keep Brutus at the focal point of the
people's wrath, so he calls special attention to one hole that has
more blood about it than the others:

> Through this the well-beloved Brutus stabb'd;
> And as he pluck'd his cursed steel away,
> Mark how the blood of Caesar follow'd it,
> As rushing out of doors, to be resolv'd
> If Brutus so unkindly knock'd or no;
> For Brutus, as you know, was Caesar's angel:
> Judge, O you gods! how dearly Caesar lov'd him.

The crowd is overcome with grief. He interrupts their wailing:

> Kind souls, what! weep you when you but behold
> Our Caesar's vesture wounded? Look you here,
> Here is himself, marr'd, as you see, with traitors.

The reaction of the crowd to the sight of the mutilated body is
terrific: "Revenge! — About! — Seek! — Burn! — Fire! — Kill! —
Slay! — Let not a traitor live!" With an effort he holds them back.
He is not yet ready to let them go. He still has to cast discredit
upon the motives of the conspirators, make sure that Brutus is
kept in the focus of their fury, provide an excuse for their gulli-
bility in allowing themselves to be convinced by Brutus, and to
project them upon a course of action:

What private griefs they have, alas; I know not,
That made them do it; they are wise and honorable,
And will no doubt with reasons answer you.
I come not, friends, to steal away your hearts:
I am no orator, as Brutus is;
But, as you know me all, a plain blunt man,
That love my friend; and that they know full well
That gave me public leave to speak of him.
For I have neither wit, nor words, nor worth,
Action, nor utterance, nor the power of speech,
To stir men's blood . . . but were I Brutus,
And Brutus Antony, there were an Antony
Would ruffle up your spirits, and put a tongue
In every wound of Caesar, that should move
The stones of Rome to rise and mutiny.

He has told them what to do, and the wild response is, "We'll mutiny!"

But he does not yet let them go. He has the means of raising their frenzy one pitch higher. He reminds them of the will that they have completely forgotten. When they hear that Caesar has left each and every one of them seventy-five drachmas and turned his estate into a public park, hell breaks loose, and the exhausted Antony can only mutter: "Mischief, thou art afoot, take thou what course thou wilt." The spirit of Caesar, in him embodied, has cried "Havoc," and let slip the dogs of war.

What a masterpiece of spellbinding! What a politician the author could have made, had he been so minded!

We next meet Mark Antony at a meeting of the Triumvirate, with Octavius and Lepidus. There he is the heartless, calculating Machiavellian. They are drawing up a proscription list. The task is complicated by the fact that among those to be liquidated are friends and relatives of one or the other of the three. Hence there must be reciprocal concession and this is granted in the most nonchalant fashion:

Antony. These many then shall die; their names are prick'd.
Octavius. Your brother too must die; consent you, Lepidus?
Lepidus. I do consent—
Octavius.   Prick him down, Antony.
Lepidus. Upon condition Publius shall not live,
Who is your sister's son, Mark Antony.
Antony. He shall not live; look, with a spot I damn him.

Octavius does not even wait for Lepidus to finish his sentence. The moment he hears the words, "I do consent," he orders Antony to "prick him down." And how nonchalantly Antony hands his sister's son over for execution!

When this unpleasant bit of routine business is disposed of, Antony sends Lepidus off to fetch Caesar's will. He frankly states his motive to be "to cut off some charge in legacies." The only part of the will that our attention has been drawn to is the one concerning the bequest to the citizens, so that now we have grave misgivings about the seventy-five drachmas each was to receive, and whose announcement proved so serviceable to Antony in his funeral oration.

Finally, we see Mark Antony on the battlefield at Philippi. He gives a command to the young Octavius, whom Cassius calls "a peevish school-boy:"

> *Antony.* Octavius, lead your battle softly on,
> Upon the left hand of the even field.
> *Octavius.* Upon the right hand, I; keep thou the left.
> *Antony.* Why do you cross me in this exigent?
> *Octavious.* I do not cross you; but I will do so.

Thus is the signal sounded for the resumption of the old process of progressive elimination. That story Shakespeare reserved for his great play, *Antony and Cleopatra.*

3. MARCUS BRUTUS

The image of Brutus which Shakespeare's audience carried away with them from a performance of *Julius Caesar,* and which we carry away with us from the high school classroom, is that of a noble-minded man, torn between two loyalties, drawn against his will into a course of action which goes painfully against his grain, who adores his wife, is a tender master, who is so greatly regarded by high and low that others impersonate him on the battlefield in order to save him from captivity. Despite recent sophisticated attempts to spoil this picture, this basic portrait must remain constant if Shakespeare is to be considered master in the exercise of his art.

At the same time, no great work of art reveals itself completely at the first view. Fuller acquaintance makes us aware of overtones and richness of detail. This fact applies particularly to the dramas of Shakespeare. However Shakespeare's process of creation be explained, his characters are human creations, not analytical constructions capable of simple analysis and justification by a cordatus. We are prone to accept them apart from their creator. In real life the longer we know a man the better we know him, yet we never know him completely. Nevertheless, one hour's acquaintance ought to suffice, except under special circumstances, to give us at least a correct impression of him. And that holds true of Shakespeare's characters.

On more intimate acquaintance Brutus becomes more complex. Unpleasant traits reveal themselves, the most important of these being a human weakness which for years held a fascination for Shakespeare because of its universality, namely, sentimentalism, or self-consciousness. Brutus embodies his most thorough study of this trait. Brutus is a good man; the trouble with him is that he knows he is good. The holier-than-thou attitude is bound to lead one into embarrassing contradictions in word and deed, and of course it does so with Brutus. It makes him ever ready to deliver long speeches. It makes him susceptible to flattery. It makes him assume that he is the leader of the conspiracy the moment he joins it, and, further, to object to anybody being admitted who would not follow him. He will not admit a great man like Cicero, who would be a pillar of strength to their cause, but does admit the insignificant Ligarius, who would follow him implicitly: "He loves me well, and I have given him reasons." He can condemn Cassius for shady practices in raising funds to carry on the war, but is indignant when he thinks that Cassius has refused to supply him with a part of those funds:

> I did send to you
> For certain sums of gold, which you denied me:
> For I can raise no money by vile means.

So blind to oneself does self-consciousness make one! One can imagine how Brutus would have felt had his attention been drawn to the damnable implication in his declaration. He is deeply affected by the death of Portia, but he cannot resist seizing the occasion to show off how philosophically he can take it. He boasts to Cassius, "No man bears sorrow better" and in a moment he finds the opportunity to prove it. Messala asks him: "Had you your letters from your wife, my lord?"

Brutus. No, Messala.
Messala. Nor nothing in your letters writ of her?
Brutus. Nothing, Messala.
Messala.   That, methinks, is strange.
Brutus. Why ask you? Hear you aught of her in yours?
Messala. No, my lord.
Brutus. Now, as you are a Roman, tell me true!
Messala. Then like a Roman bear the truth I tell:
For certain she is dead, and by strange manner.
Brutus. Why, farewell, Portia. We must die, Messala:
With meditating that she must die once,
I have the patience to endure it now.

This is play-acting of the cheapest variety but he craved the admiration of Messala, expressed in the words, "Even so great men great losses should endure," and especially that of Cassius, for whose particular benefit he put on this act. The latter's declaration:

> I have as much of this in art as you,
> But yet my nature could not bear it so,

is the compliment he was angling for.

Another unflattering trait that we discover in Brutus, and which helps to account for some of his inconsistent behavior, is an inability to reason logically. He speaks confidently of giving satisfactory reasons for the assassination, and thinks that he has proved that Caesar was ambitious; whereas all he has done is repeat the assumption. He sets out to prove to himself that Caesar ought to be killed. Accordingly, he begins with the conclusion: "It must be by his death" and before he is through he has made out a pretty good case for sparing him. Caesar is to be slain, then, not for what he has done, but for what he *might* do. A curious code of criminal law! He admits that he has never known the time when Caesar's conduct was determined by his emotion rather than his reason. Not many of us can boast of acquaintances of whom that might be affirmed. If that were true of Caesar, then he was the man to be entrusted with power. He advances a pretentious argument for sparing Antony, and succeeds in making out a perfect case for killing him. Antony is but a limb of Caesar, he argues, so what is the use of cuttting off the limb when the head is off? They are after the spirit of Caesar, not the body.

What, then, is the use of hacking the body, like butchers? The poor man cannot perceive that if their aim were to kill the body of Caesar, then cutting off the head would suffice; but if it is the destruction of the spirit of Caesar, then every limb in which that spirit might reside must be removed—and Brutus recognized Antony as a limb of Caesar. He prides himself on effecting a subtle tactical stroke when he insists that Antony speak *after* him. There is ironic humor in Antony's mock-humble acquiescence: "Be it so; I do desire no more." But Brutus has no sense of humor. Otherwise, he would not be so self-conscious.

Brutus considers himself a philosopher, but he has the temperament of a poet. He reasons in images: the ladder of ambition, the serpent in the shell, the headless trunk, the tide in the affairs of men. Analogies built on such images lead him to fatal action. He is even confused about what he is fighting for. In a vague way he realizes that Caesar is a menace to the republic whose institutions must be dear to him, as traditional institutions always are to those who enjoy their benefits. His ancestors had driven out the Tarquins; hence, he could not be happy at the thought of a return to monarchy. Yet we find him ready to yield Caesar the crown if he were quite sure that he would not abuse his power as king. Later we hear him say:

> What! shall one of us,
> That struck the foremost man of all this world
> But for supporting robbers, shall we now
> contaminate our fingers with base bribes . . . ?

Just why *did* he kill Caesar? In short, Brutus was a confused man, who had no business in the world of practical affairs. He should have stayed in his study, where he would not be called upon to decide practical issues, where his ideals would not be forced to clash with unlovely realities. And there he would have stayed had not Cassius cleverly drawn him out. He would have suffered in helpless silence, like his numerous counterparts in many corners of the world today.

Brutus has been thoughtlessly compared to the zealous reformer, who today succeeds in upsetting a corrupt administration, only, in the end, to demonstrate his own ineptitude. Far from being the reformer, he is the rigid conservative, if not reactionary, the defender of things as they are, stubbornly shutting his eyes to

the inequities which eventually must start rolling the wave of
rebellion, on whose crest rides a Caesar. Characteristically, he
never learns the truth. Though he lost the fight, he dies happy in
the thought that the fight was for the right. History will be the
judge:

> I shall have glory by this losing day,
> More than Octavius and Mark Antony
> By this vile conquest shall attain unto.

4. CAIUS CASSIUS

"Must I endure all this?" implores the outraged Cassius. "All
this; ay, more!" has been the relentless answer. Time seems to
have set no limit to what Cassius must endure. Not only has he
been generally considered the villian of the play, but every once
in a while a commentator startles us with a fresh discovery of
some specific variety of turpitude. Thus, Mr. Percy Simpson finds
him to be theatrical. To be sure, now and then an interpreter
comes forward with a good word for the wretch; but the praise
thus given is apt to be of the faint variety that damns. What the
traditional attitude has been may be inferred from a statement of
the case, made by a secondary school teacher, in a periodical
conducted by and for secondary school teachers—in other words,
those to whom is entrusted the molding of literary judgments. In
the May, 1936 issue of *High Points,* published in New York, is an
article on the teaching of *Julius Caesar,* we read this:

The second type [previously described as those self-seekers who find
their political careers nipped in the bud] is found in Cassius, a politi-
cally ambitious revolutionary, anxious to rid Rome of Caesar for his
own personal advancement . . .
    When we regard Cassius as the shrewd self-seeeker, which he actu-
ally was under the guise of being an idealistic opponent of the evils
of the regimes, we cannot help bringing to light his modern analogues,
the Capones, and the Schultzes, who, like Cassius, employ dull-witted
henchmen to carry out crimes which they plan, and who indulge in
all the clever subtleties of the criminal mind. It is interesting to watch
Cassius, who could easily have earned a comfortable living in 1935 by
conducting a course in 'How to consummate successful conspiracies,
in 10 easy lessons.'

What confused rubbish! Nobody ever realized before that the Capones and the Schultzes had frustrated political ambitions, or that Cassius' fellow conspirators were dull-witted henchmen.

The kind of man Shakespeare intended Cassius to be is no mystery. The material for judging him is all there in the play, plain as can be, and the interpretation of the material encounters little difficulty. How so distorted a view of one of Shakespeare's noblest characters could ever have been adopted and fostered is puzzling—but not inexplicable. Before presenting the explanation I shall analyze the data which Shakespeare gives us for the formation of a judgment. To begin with, everybody in the play except Caesar thinks well of Cassius. When Caesar confides his misgivings concerning Cassius to Antony, the latter reassures him:

> Fear him not, Caesar; he's not dangerous;
> He is a noble Roman and well given.

Nobody doubts Antony's ability to judge human nature. His slave has respect and affection for him. When Brutus, with a woeful lack of dignity, complains to Pindarus:

> Your master, Pindarus,
> In his own charge, or by ill officers,
> Hath given me some worthy cause to wish
> Things done, undone: but, if he be at hand,
> I shall be satisfied,

the latter returns the proud retort:

> I do not doubt
> But that my noble master will appear
> Such as he is—full of regard and honor;

And when he has stabbed Cassius at the latter's command, his words are:

> So I am free; yet would not so have been,
> Durst I have done my will.

Titinius, finding Cassius dead, mourns:

> Cassius is no more. O setting sun,
> As in thy red rays thou dost sink to night,
> So in his red blood Cassius' day is set;

The sun of Rome is set! ...
Why didst thou send me forth, brave Cassius? ...
Alas, thou hast misconstrued everything!
But hold thee; take this garland on thy brow;
Thy Brutus bid me give it thee, and I
Will do his bidding. Brutus, come apace,
And see how I regarded Caius Cassius.
By your leave, gods: this is a Roman's part:
Come, Cassius' sword, and find Titinius' heart.

When Brutus arrives on the spot, he exclaims:

The last of all the Romans, fare thee well!
It is impossible that ever Rome
Should breed thy fellow. Friends, I owe more tears
To this dead man than you shall see me pay.
I shall find time, Cassius, I shall find time.

There is no ambiguity about these utterances. They prove
Cassius to be a noble, highly regarded character. If there were
anything in the play to prove that he is an envious, self-seeking
politician, there would be a bald inconsistency—there would be
something wrong with the play.

Of course, Cassius has his faults. Caesar tells us that he loves
no plays, and hears no music, and seldom smiles—serious offenses,
granted, but not criminal offenses. Puritans are guilty of these
offenses—and saints might be. They may be corollary to an uncompromising sincerity, such as implied in Cassius' challenge
to Brutus:

Were I a common laugher, or did use
To stale with ordinary oaths my love
To every new protester; if you do know
That I do fawn on men and hug them hard
And after scandal them, or if you know
That I profess myself in banqueting
To all the rout, then hold me dangerous.

Caesar also complains of Cassius that—

He thinks too much: such men are dangerous;
.... he reads much;
He is a great observer, and he looks
Quite through the deeds of men.

We admire men who think much, and read much, and can see through the deeds of men to their motives. It is Caesar, not Cassius, that is here arraigned. He has reason to fear such a man.

What can we infer from the conduct of Cassius in the play? We are introduced to him when he attempts to persuade Brutus to join a conspiracy which he has already organized, whose object is the assassination of Julius Caesar. He proves to be a shrewd manipulator of men, and at the end of the interview we are sure that Brutus will join.

We next see him on the eve of the assassination. He there rises to heroic proportions. There is a cataclysm in nature, and he feels himself in harmony with the furious forces thus set loose. He goes about the streets with his breast bared, in defiance of the thunderstorm. He is convinced that the "strange impatience of the heavens" proves that the gods have made his cause their own. His alertness is in evidence. He recognizes Casca by his voice, and Cinna by his gait, and he succeeds in winning a new recruit in Casca, at this, the eleventh hour. Taking this new recruit along he makes his way, with his fellow-conspirators, to Brutus' house, where Brutus formally joins them. At that moment Cassius drops into a subordinate position, deferring to the new leader, Brutus, even when the latter's ruling was contrary to his own better judgment. He organized the conspiracy, but it was never his intention to assume leadership. He was interested in the cause, not himself, and that, to him, was entitled to a greater man than he for standard-bearer. He turned to Brutus, but had always had his eye on Cicero, a still greater personality. When Casca reports on the attempted crowning of Caesar, he eagerly demands to know if Cicero said anything. Now that Brutus has been won over, he suggests that they approach Cicero. The suggestion is greeted by a chorus of approval. But Brutus vetoes the suggestion: Cicero is not a man that will follow, he avers. As pointed out above, the moment he joins, he considers himself the leader.

Nevertheless, it is not long before Cassius is called back, at least for a moment, to seize the helm to save their cause from going on the rocks.

The first few minutes following the assassination constitute, of course, an extremely critical period. How does Brutus measure up to the crisis? Does he behave like the leader of a great cause, the success of which now hangs in the balance, or like the man

who has just murdered his friend—"a dreadful thing," as he himself calls the act? The answer is that he behaves like the man who
has just murdered his friend.

When Metellus advises, "Stand fast together," Brutus exclaims,
"Talk not of standing"—and remains standing. Presently Trebon-
ius re-enters with the report that

> Men, wives and children stare, cry out and run
> As it were doomsday—

and Brutus resigns himself to utter despair:

> Fates, we will know your pleasures!
> That we shall die, we know; 'tis but the time
> And drawing days out, that men stand upon.

Cassius, realizing how fraught with danger is this state of mind,
promptly seeks to use Brutus' own thought to minimize the seriousness of the assassination:

> Why, he that cuts off twenty years of life
> Cuts off so many years of fearing death.

Brutus snatches at the suggestion, and elaborates it with the
eagerness—and the simplicity—of a child:

> Grant that, and then is death a benefit:
> So are we Caesar's frends, that have abridg'd
> His time of fearing death.

Stirred from his apathy he calls to his companions:

> Stoop, Romans, stoop,
> And let us bathe our hands in Caesar's blood
> Up to our elbows, and besmear our swords:
> Then walk we forth, even to the market-place,
> And, waving our red weapons o'er our heads,
> Let's all cry "Peace, freedom, and liberty!"

Here Cassius exclaims:

> How many ages hence
> Shall this our lofty scene be acted o'er
> In states unborn and accents yet unknown—

in which Shakespeare foretells his own play.

This is the speech which prompted Mr. Percy Simpson to declare: "It is not the only passage in which Shakespeare has given a touch of pose, of theatricality, to the character of Cassius." Mr. Simpson assumes here a novel position. It is commonly held, I believe, that it is Brutus who is given the touch of pose, in contrast with Cassius. Mr. Simpson has simply failed to take into consideration the occasion and the purpose of the speech. The course of action recommended by Brutus has more than a mere touch of pose and theatricality, but his mind is now traveling in a safe direction, so Cassius seeks to encourage him in his present train of thought. It happens that he has miscalculated and touched the wrong chord, for what Brutus is impressed with is the difference, not the similarity, between the image painted by Cassius and the present situation. In the former the assassination was merely make-believe—"sport,"whereas in the latter Caesar was really dead. To recover the ground lost, Cassius hastens to urge the impression which that play-acting would make upon posterity. It would bring glory to the memory of Brutus and his companions. They would be called "the men that gave their country liberty." When, finally, the ever ready Decius comes to the rescue with his question, "What, shall we forth?" Cassius answers decisively:

> Ay, every man away.
> *Brutus shall lead,* and we will grace his heels
> With the boldest and best hearts of Rome—

thus making a final desperate effort to shake Brutus out of his daze, and brace him up. Presently we see him making a vain attempt to prevent Brutus from permitting Antony to speak to the people. Brutus, of course, knows better, and insists on the fatal move; so that the next time we see them together their nerves are frayed by impending disaster, and we have the quarrel scene in which Cassius at last gives vent to his pent-up feelings, and tells Brutus to his face that he does not know how to manage things. Only once again does he permit himself to allude to Brutus' inefficiency: namely, during the parley in the last act, when Antony calls them flatterers. "Flatterers!" exclaims the indignant Cassius:

> Now, Brutus, thank yourself:
> This tongue had not offended so today
> If Cassius might have rul'd.

After the quarrel Cassius learns of the death of Portia. He is
horror-stricken. He is so free from self-consciousness that he believes that the guilt for the altercation rests solely on him, and he
exclaims, "How 'scap'd I killing when I crossed you so!" Brutus
calls for wine:

> *Brutus.* In this I bury all unkindness, Cassius.
> *Cassius.* My heart is thirsty for that noble pledge.
> Fill, Lucius, till the wine o'erswell the cup;
> I cannot drink too much of Brutus' love.

Even after they have settled down to business with Titinius and
Messala, he cannot forget Portia, and Brutus has to beg him to
desist. This is the touching dialogue with which they part for the
night:

> *Brutus.*   Noble, noble Cassius,
> Good night, and good repose.
> *Cassius.*   O my dear brother!
> This was an ill beginning of the night:
> Never come such division 'tween our souls!
> Let it not, Brutus.

Cassius' affection and regard for Brutus are again brought out
on the battlefield. When Octavius declares that he was not born
to die on Brutus' sword, Cassius calls him "a peevish schoolboy,
worthless of such honor." On his last appearance in the play both
his manliness and his nobility of soul are made manifest. He
enters carrying the ensign, and exclaims:

> O, look, Titinius, look, the villains fly!
> Myself have to mine own turn'd enemy:
> This ensign here of mine was turning back!
> I slew the coward and did take it from him.

He sends Titinius on a mission—apparently to his death. That is
more than Cassius is willing to outlive:

> O! coward that I am, to live so long,
> To see my best friend ta'en before my face!

He acts the Roman's part and falls upon his sword.

I submit that the man who emerges from these lines and situations is a noble, high-minded character. There can be no two

views on the subject. How, then, could so unfavorable a view of Cassius come to prevail? A popular proverb gives us a hint of the process. If we give a dog a bad name the hanging becomes a matter of course. Let us ignore for the moment the question of how the bad name came to be attached to Cassius. It is evident that once we think ill of him our minds will be closed to contradicting evidence, and we shall interpret everything he says and does in the light (or the shadow) of our prejudice. For instance, to many it seems clear that when Cassius advances Caesar's behaving like a sick girl when he was in a fever, and calling for help when he was drowning, as illustrations of his inferiority, he is actuated by envy. To the modern mind there is nothing reprehensible in showing weakness in a fever, or in calling for help when drowning. But a Roman might well be amazed that

> A man of such a feeble temper should
> So get the start of the majestic world,

and hold dictatorial power over his betters. Cassius would rather have gone down than called for help from the man he had challenged. In addition, it must not be overlooked that, under the circumstances, when he was doing his best to win Brutus over to his cause, Cassius would not have used these illustrations, had he not known that Brutus, as a Roman, would agree with him.

Again, he is accused of instilling the anti-Caesar poison into Brutus' mind. The fact is that the poison has been there for some time, and apparently developed there naturally. He was as much opposed to a dictatorship as Cassius, only he was the type of man, as indicated above, to suffer in apparent apathy. He needed a man like Cassius to rouse him to action. From the workings of that poison he has been neglecting his friends, has been struggling with conflicting emotions ("vexed with passions of some difference," as he expresses it). It makes him unwilling to witness the ceremonies in honor of his best friend, Caesar, and he refuses to go to them even after Cassius urges him to go. It is Brutus, not Cassius, who first hints at Caesar's ambition:

> What means this shouting? I do fear the people
> Choose Caesar for their king.

This spontaneous admission of fear serves Cassius as a cue, and he proceeds with his so-called "seduction." Before he can come to the point, however, Brutus anticipates him:

> What you would work me to, I have some aim:
> How I have thought of this and of these times,
> I shall recount hereafter.

Similarly, and with a charming disregard of the text, is the famous quarrel scene perverted to represent a clash between the noble, long-suffering Brutus and the ignoble, nagging Cassius. What the play really presents is something very nearly the opposite. Brutus is impatiently waiting for Cassius to arrive in order to berate him for not sending him money he had requested. But Cassius too has a grievance, namely, that Brutus has ignored his intercession on behalf of Lucius Pella, and can hardly wait till he come face to face with Brutus to charge him home with what he considers an affront. He thus takes an unexpected offensive. This offensive, however, he holds for only a few lines. When Brutus advances the opinion that Cassius wronged himself to intercede in such a case, Cassius very properly urges that

> In such a time as this it is not meet
> That every nice offense should bear his comment.

Brutus does not even deign to answer this excellent argument but, instead, hurls a personal insult at Cassius. From this moment Cassius is on the defensive, writhing piteously under repeated blows, and exercising incredible self-control. When he declares:

> You know that you are Brutus that speaks this,
> Or, by the gods, this speech were else your last—

does anybody doubt that he means what he says? Can there be any doubt what would be the outcome of a physical encounter between the two men? Yet Cassius takes insult after insult, vainly imploring Brutus to desist, and not to presume too much upon his love. That love proves strong enough to restrain him from doing that which he should be sorry for. Since Brutus maintains the offensive, he is in a position to terminate the quarrel whenever he pleases, and Cassius gives him several excellent opportunities to do so. For instance, when Brutus charges him: "You say you are a better soldier: let it appear so," at the same time injecting an insult, Cassius shuts his ears to the insult, and appealing corrects him:

> You wrong me every way; you wrong me, Brutus;
> I said an elder soldier, not a better;
> Did I say better?

Brutus' curt rebuff is, "If you did, I care not."

When Brutus upbraids Cassius for denying him the money he had sent for, Cassius vehemently declares: "I denied you not ... He was but a fool that brought my answer back." At this point the natural thing for Brutus to do is to ask, "What *was* your answer?" Instead, he simply ignores what Cassius has said, and prosecutes the dissension with a grand assumption of self-righteousness, finding repeated opportunity to vaunt his own superior virtue.

When the quarrel finally ends—for no particular reason, except that it had to come to an end some time—Cassius (who has not that exalted opinion of his own goodness which makes Brutus take advantage of every opportunity to speak well of himself) ingenuously assumes that he has been to blame—and Brutus magnanimously forgives him. Shakespeare comprehended the complexity of human nature.

I am aware that I am likely to be accused of deliberately overlooking two passages that do not jibe well with my thesis. I have not overlooked them; I have merely reserved them. One of them is Mark Antony's last speech, glorifying Brutus:

> This was the noblest Roman of them all:
> All the conspirators, save only he,
> Did that they did in envy of great Caesar;
> He only, in a general honest thought,
> And common good to all, made one of them.

Here is the explanation for the prevailing view of Cassius' character. The high school graduate has memorized this speech, and has never thought of questioning the truth of what it affirms. The statement is definite—no two ways of reading it. But it directly contradicts the rest of the play. So we have to choose: which shall be accepted as authoritative of Shakespeare's intention—the play, or a single short passage which might be omitted without leaving a gap? It is discrepancies such as the one afforded by this passage that men like Fleay and Robertson consider proof of multiplicity of hands in the writing of the play. I do not think it necessary to look upon Antony's encomium as a patch or an interpolation. It would be quite in keeping with Shakespeare's method for him to sacrifice consistency to his immediate purpose. What he was interested in at this point was to wind up the play on an optimistic note, as he customarily does in his tragedies. Antony's remarks smooth the way conveniently for the closing lines, spoken by Octavius, the last words of which, let us remember, are:

> . . . and let's away
> To part the glories of this *happy* day.

Absorbed in his purpose, Shakespeare mechanically followed Plutarch, in whom we read:

It was said that Antonius spake it openly divers times, that he thought that of all them that had slain Caesar, there was none but Brutus only that was moved to do it as thinking the act commendable of itself: but that all the other conspirators did conspire his death for some private malice or envy that they otherwise did bear unto him.

If Shakespeare became at all aware of the possible incongruity he was creating, he could dismiss it with the thought that Antony would naturally hold the opinion he was expressing, and that the audience was not being called upon to see Cassius through Antony's eyes.

The other passage that I have reserved occurs in the first act, in Cassius' soliloquy following the instigation of Brutus. It offers a less simple problem:

> Well, Brutus, thou art noble; yet, I see,
> Thy honorable metal may be wrought
> From that it is dispos'd: therefore 'tis meet
> That noble minds keep ever with their likes;
> For who so firm that cannot be seduc'd?
> Caesar doth bear me hard; but he loves Brutus:
> If I were Brutus now and he were Cassius,
> He should not humor me.

This sounds very much like a confession on Cassius' part that he knows that he is performing an ignoble act. But is that a necessary implication? All he admits is that if he loved Caesar he could not be brought to join a conspiracy against him. In other words, if he had to choose between love and duty he would choose love. Are we sure that he is wrong? Love is a fact; duty is a matter of opinion. Brutus chose duty, and we know that he chose wrong.

Perhaps the lesson of the play lies in just that. Recent history affords examples of countries in which the children were taught that it was their duty to betray their parents—much to the revulsion of the rest of the world. What friendship meant to the ancient Roman cannot be too strongly impressed upon us. When Cassius believes that he has sent his friend Titinius to his death, he commits suicide. Titinius does the same when he finds that Cassius has killed himself for his sake, his dying words being, "By your leave, gods; this is a Roman's part." And we may recall that when Hamlet is dying, his friend Horatio tries to follow him, declaring, "I am more an antique Roman than a Dane." In Shakespeare only a villain like Edmund can place loyalty to state even above loyalty to his father.

At any rate, the two passages just cited go a long way toward explaining the opprobrium attaching to Cassius. Near the beginning of the play we seem to be told by Cassius himself that he is a villain, and at the end we are very definitely told by Antony that he is. Yet there is not the slightest evidence that he has any selfish or otherwise dishonorable motive. He wishes the conspiracy to succeed. To that end, being a practical politician, he resorts to ways and means dictated by success. He seeks to enlist the best men he can reach—a Brutus, a Cicero—men who must inevitably cast him in the shade. But that does not matter to him. It is Brutus that objects to admitting men who might supersede him. He is impelled by the same motives as actuate Flavius and Marullus and Brutus. They all are bent on forestalling the "hard conditions as this time is like to lay upon" them, as Brutus expresses it. Or as Cassius puts it at the end of the very soliloquy which is cited against him: "For we will shake him [Caesar] or worse days endure." This is not said to impress anybody; he is talking to himself. There is really no problem here. The interests of his class are jeopardized, the political ideals that he and his ancestors have cherished are in danger of subversion, and he is so constituted that he cannot remain apathetic. That is all there is to it. His formation of the conspiracy does not make him out to be either a good man or a bad man. It has no bearing on his moral make-up. That is revealed in other ways—and I have tried to show what it is. We may find that his standards are not as lofty as those of Brutus, that he is guided by expediency, that he does not scruple to resort to questionable means to bring about what he considers an honorable end, that he loves no plays, hears no music, and seldom smiles—but, when all is said and done, the very head and front of his offending has this extent—and no more.

Now let us turn to Shakespeare himself for a statement of his intention. In *Antony and Cleopatra*, the sequel to *Julius Caesar*, we read:

> What was't
> That mov'd pale Cassius to conspire? and what
> Made the all-honor'd honest Roman, Brutus,
> With the arm'd rest, courtiers of beauteous freedom,
> To drench the Capitol, but that they would
> Have one man but a man?

CHAPTER 4

Shakespeare The Preacher:
A Study of Macbeth

"**F**OR WHAT SHALL it profit a man if he shall gain the whole world, and lose his own soul?" With this appropriate text I can imagine the preacher William Shakespeare introducing his sermon. From there he proceeds to narrate the parable of Macbeth, the man of noble potentialities, with the capacity and the opportunity to enjoy those things that give meaning to life, yet who so conducted himself that, in the end, life had lost all meaning for him. But the figure of Shakespeare standing in the pulpit is only an image in my own mind. Shakespeare was not a clerk in holy orders. He was a writer of plays, and as such he performed his function, as he himself proclaimed, by visual presentation "to hold, as 'twere, the mirror up to nature; to show virtue her own feature, scorn her own image, and the very age and body of the time his form and pressure." If the mirror he held up reflected life truthfully, then the resulting play might teach a lesson, for life is the most inexorable of teachers, and in that sense might be called a sermon. The lesson taught by *Macbeth* is aptly expressed in the Biblical text quoted.

Robert Browning gave it as his opinion that a poet should be interested in "incidents in the development of a soul," and further, that "little else is worth study." He did not specify the direction of development. The tragedy *Macbeth* affords an opportunity to inquire into incidents in the deterioration of a soul.

Accompanied by Banquo, Macbeth returns from the battlefield, a conquering hero, crowned with glory, rich in "golden opinions." The two are confronted by three women, described as witches in the stage direction, but never so called in Shakespeare's text. There they are called "weird sisters," which leads us to suspect that the poet meant to endow them with a dignity above the popular conception of a witch. They greet Macbeth:

1. Witch. All hail, Macbeth! hail to thee, Thane of Glamis!
2. Witch. All hail, Macbeth! hail to thee, Thane of Cawdor!
3. Witch. All hail, Macbeth, that shalt be king hereafter!

At the third greeting Macbeth starts violently, so much so that Banquo is prompted to ask:

> Good sir, why do you start, and seem to fear
> Things that do sound so fair?

But Macbeth is too deeply absorbed to answer. Obviously he is frightened because the prophecy awakened a guilty thought dormant in his subconsciousness. Receiving no reply Banquo turns to the weird sisters and challenges them to reveal what the future has in store for him. They prophesy that though he will never be king, he will be ancestor to a line of kings, whereupon they vanish. Macbeth, now aroused, calls frantically after them, "Tell me more . . ."Would they had stay'd!" If they had only told him how his ascent to the throne would come about! At this point Ross and Angus arrive with the news that the king had bestowed the title of Thane of Cawdor upon Macbeth. At this quick and stunning confirmation of one of the prophecies Macbeth mutters: "Glamis, and Thane of Cawdor! The greatest is behind" and turning to Banquo he asks:

> Do you not hope your children shall be kings,
> When those that gave the Thane of Cawdor to me
> Promis'd no less to them?
>   *Banquo.*   That trusted home,
> Might yet enkindle you unto the crown,
> Besides the Thane of Cawdor.

Then he issues this grave warning!

>   But 'tis strange;
> And oftentimes, to win us to our harm,
> The instruments of darkness tell us truths,
> Win us with honest trifles, to betray's
> In deepest consequence.

Banquo finds, however, that he is talking to the air; Macbeth has not heard him. He is sunk in a deep reverie, oblivious of the company present. His friend Banquo, to ease the embarrassment, engages the messengers in a separate conversation, leaving Macbeth rapt in his own thoughts:

> Two truths are told,
> As happy prologues to the swelling act
> Of the imperial theme . . .
> This supernatural soliciting
> Cannot be ill—cannot be good. If ill,
> Why hath it given me earnest of success,
> Commencing in a truth? I'm thane of Cawdor.
> If good, why do I yield to that suggestion
> Whose horrid image doth unfix my hair,
> And make my seated heart knock at my ribs,
> Against the use of nature? Present fears
> Are less than horrible imaginings.
> My thought, whose murder yet is but fantastical,
> Shakes so my single state of man that function
> Is smother'd in surmise, and nothing is
> But what is not.

Now we know, we do not have to surmise, what made him startle at the witch's prophecy. He could not dissociate his ascent to the throne from the act of murder. The answer to the first question he would have found in Banquo's warning, which he did not hear because of his absorption.

He pauses for a while in silent meditation, and then comes out with this wise decision: "If chance will have me king, why chance may crown me." Had he stopped there he would have been safe. But his mind keeps on working back and forth, till he finally arrives at this indecisive conclusion:

> Come what come may,
> Time and the hour runs through the roughest day.

And we know that he is tangled up and lost in the web of fate. On which side the beam of his intention was inclining at this moment in his cogitation we can gather when he renews his conversation with Banquo:

> *Macbeth.* Think upon what hath chanc'd, and, at more time,
> The interim having weigh'd it, let us speak
> Our free hearts each to other.
> *Banquo.*   Very gladly.
> *Macbeth.* Till then, enough.

Had he been inclined to leave the ordering of events to chance, there would have been no occasion for a conference with Banquo, or anybody else,

In the meantime, at the palace, King Duncan receives the report of the execution of the traitor Cawdor, and his comment is:

> There's no art
> To find the mind's construction in the face.
> He was a gentleman on whom I built
> An absolute trust—

He is interrupted by the entrance of Macbeth, his prospective murderer, on whom he is at this very moment building an absolute trust—a fine example of dramatic irony. The irony is immediately repeated in Macbeth's address to the king:

> . . . our duties
> Are to your throne and state, children and servants,
> Which do but what they should, by doing everything
> Safe toward your love and honor.

At the moment he probably sincerely means what he says, as he does not much later, when he repeats an echo of this sentiment.

King Duncan is in a buoyant mood after Macbeth's military victory. To signalize the occasion he does something that must perforce accelerate Macbeth's drift toward direct action: he nominates his eldest son Prince of Cumberland, which makes him heir apparent. Macbeth soliloquizes:

> The Prince of Cumberland! That is a step
> On which I must fall down, or else o'erleap,
> For in my way it lies. Stars, hide your fires;
> Let not light see my black and deep desires;
> The eye wink at the hand; yet let that be
> Which the eye fears, when it is done, to see.

As the king announces his intention to proceed to Macbeth's castle, Macbeth takes leave to prepare for his reception:

> I'll be myself the harbinger and make joyful
> The hearing of my wife with your approach.

Dramatic irony again: Lady Macbeth will certainly be made joyful!

Macbeth had already made the hearing of his wife joyful, not indeed with the news of the king's coming, but with the report of the Weird Sisters' prophecy. He would not keep her waiting. He loves his wife, loves her dearly. He never once addresses her directly except in terms of endearment. He despatches a letter with this explanation:

This have I thought good to deliver theee, my dearest partner of greatness, that thou might'st not lose the dues of rejoicing by being ignorant of what greatness is promis'd thee.

"What greatness is promis'd *thee*," not *me*, not even *us*, but *thee*. Lady Macbeth, on the other hand, thinks primarily of the greatness promised her husband:

> Hie thee hither
> That I may pour my spirits in thine ear,
> And chastise with the valor of my tongue
> All that impedes thee from the golden round
> Which fate and metaphysical aid doth seem
> To have thee crown'd withal.

She is impatient for the fulfilment of the prophecy; but she is afraid that there is too much of the milk of human kindness in his composition for him "to catch the nearest way." We get from the wife an expert analysis of the husband's character:

> Thou wouldst be great,
> Art not without ambition, but without
> The illness should attend it. What thou wouldst highly,
> That wouldst thou holily; wouldst not play false,
> And yet wouldst wrongly win. Thou'dst have, great Glamis,
> That which cries, "Thus must thou do, if thou have it;"
> And that which rather thou dost fear to do
> Than wishest should be undone.

She therefore decides to take the matter into her own hands:

> Come, you spirits
> That tend on mortal thoughts, unsex me here,
> And fill me from the crown to the toe top-full
> Of direst cruelty! Make thick my blood;
> Stop up th'access and passage to remorse,
> That no conpunctions visitings of nature
> Shake my fell purpose, nor keep peace between
> Th'effect and it! Come to my woman's breasts
> And take my milk for gall, you murd'ring ministers,
> Wherever in your sightless substances
> You wait on nature's mischief! Come, thick night,
> And pall thee in the dunnest smoke of hell

> That my keen knife see not the wound it makes,
> Nor heaven peep through the blanket of the dark
> To cry, "Hold, hold!"

This amazing conjuration makes it clear that Lady Macbeth did not feel herself lacking in that "milk of human kindness" which she attributes an excess of to her husband. Nevertheless when Macbeth arrives and she finds him hesitant, she tells him firmly:

> ... you shall put
> This night's great business into my dispatch,
> Which shall to all our nights and days to come
> Give solely sovereign sway and masterdom.

This woman, then, who has evidently been Macbeth's partner in a happy union of whom he dreams as his "dearest partner of greatness," is about to become his bloody partner in a ghastly nightmare of guilt.

When the royal party arrives, Lady Macbeth receives it in regal fashion. We can understand her lofty ambition. It cannot be denied that she is fit to be queen. Macbeth is not on the scene. We must imagine that he could not bring himself to face the king. He even withdraws from the supper table. We find him alone with his thoughts. We are not surprised to find that he has canceled his wife's humiliating determination to take the whole affair out of his hands. After all, he is a soldier, and a brave one. But he has a conscience, and it does not let him rest:

> He's here in double trust:
> First as I am his kinsman and his subject,
> Strong both against the deed; then as his host,
> Who should against his murderer shut the door,
> Not bear the knife myself.

Besides, there is danger of retribution—not in the next world— he would risk that—but right here in this world:

> Besides, this Duncan
> Hath borne his faculties so meek, hath been
> So clear in his great office, that his virtues
> Will plead like angels, trumpet-tongu'd, against
> The deep damnation of his taking-off;

He ends his deliberation on a note of helplessness:

> I have no spur
> To prick the sides of my intent, but only
> Vaulting ambition.

He has made up his mind. He will be content with the honor and glory he has already achieved:

> He hath honored me of late; and I have bought
> Golden opinions from all sorts of people,
> Which would be worn now in their newest gloss,
> Not cast aside so soon.

When his wife appears he tells her with decision: "We will proceed no further in this business." Her terrific personality, however, is overwhelming. Her persuasion makes him burst out in admiration:

> Bring forth men children only;
> For thy undauted mettle should compose
> Nothing but males.

He has become a child in her hands. Fatuously he asks, as if it were an observation calling for superior perception:

> Will it not be receiv'd,
> When we have mark'd with blood those sleepy two
> Of his own chamber and us'd their very daggers,
> That they have done it?

In his bewildered state she has succeeded in making him believe that it was he who had broached the plan of murder, and the strongest move in her strategy was to suggest that his fickleness now might be taken as a measure of the strength of the love he bore her. His surrender is complete:

> I am settled, and bend up
> Each corporal agent to this terrible feat.

On his way to the king's bedchamber he encounters Banquo. Banquo is very sleepy, but he is afraid to go to bed. He cannot shake off "cursed thoughts." He remembers Macbeth's unnatural behavior when the Weird Sisters hailed him king to be, and now Duncan is within his castle. Without making any specific reference, Macbeth darkly approaches him with the proposition that if he goes along with him when the time comes, it will "make honor" for him. Banquo understands him well, and returns a straightforward answer:

> So I lose none
> In seeking to augment it, but still keep
> My bosom franchis'd and allegiance clear,
> I shall be counsell'd.

Macbeth's reply is: "Good repose the while!" Presumably, "good repose the while" may be taken as a euphemistic equivalent to the modern popular expression, "good night," delivered with an ominous intonation. Macbeth now knows Banquo's position, and realizes that it is something that he will have to take into account some day.

He waits for the signal from his wife that the grooms attending the king are asleep and the daggers in place. His whole being is in tumult. His heat-oppressed brain flashes a dagger before him pointing the way to his victim. The ground he is to tread he adjures:

> Thou sure and firm set earth,
> Hear not my steps, which way they walk, for fear
> The very stones prate of my whereabout
> And take the present horror from the time,
> Which now suits with it—The bell invites me.
> Hear it not, Duncan, for it is a knell
> That summons thee to heaven or to hell.

When he is gone Lady Macbeth appears. She is in a state of feverish agitation. She jumps at every sound. She has made the grooms drunk, and fortified her own courage with drink. When she placed the daggers ready for her husband she was in a position to carry out her original intention of murdering Duncan herself. She would have done it she says, but that the king in his sleep bore a resemblance to her own father. The woman who had asseverated,

> I have given suck, and know
> How tender 'tis to love the babe that milks me;
> I would, while it was smiling in my face,
> Have pluck'd my nipples from his boneless gums
> And dash'd the brains out, had I so sworn as you
> Have done to this,

could not bring herself to stab the man she wanted dead, merely because he resembled her father. Macbeth returns, the bloody daggers in his hands. "I have done the deed." He is a shattered man. His speech lacks sequence. He has heard noises, and he still hears them. He looks at his gory hands: "This is a sorry sight." Lady Macbeth must come to her husband's support in this mental crisis: "A foolish thought, to say a sorry sight."

> *Macbeth*. There's one did laugh in's sleep, and one cried, "Murder!"
> That they did wake each other. I stood and heard them;
> But they did say their prayers, and address'd them
> Again to sleep.
>   *Lady M*. There are two lodg'd together,
>   *Macb*. One cried "God bless us!" and "Amen" the other,
> As they had seen me with these hangman's hands.
> List'ning their fear, I could not say "Amen"
> When they did say "God bless us!"

The frightened wife exclaims: "Consider it not so deeply!"

> *Macb*. But wherefore could not I pronounce "Amen"?
> I had most need of blessing, and "Amen"
> Stuck in my throat.

The impact of the situation upon Lady Macbeth may be judged by her terrified exclamation:

> These deeds must not be thought
> After these ways; so, it will make us mad!
>   *Macb*. Methought I heard a voice cry, "Sleep no more!
> Macbeth does murder sleep." . . .
> Still it cried, "Sleep no more!" to all the house;
> Glamis hath murder'd sleep, and therefore Cawder
> Shall sleep no more; Macbeth shall sleep no more."
>   *Lady M*. Who was it that thus cried?

But now she recovers a grip upon herself, and makes an effort to rescue her husband from his despair, which, as she concedes, must lead to madness:

> Why, worthy thane,
> You do unbend your noble strength, to think
> So brainsickly of things. Go get some water,
> And wash this filthy witness from your hand.

Twice before Macbeth has called attention to the blood upon his
hands, yet Lady Macbeth's condition was such that she did not
see that he was holding the daggers. At last she is aware of them:

> Why did you bring those daggers from the place?
> They must lie there. Go carry them, and smear
> The sleepy grooms with blood.
>   *Macb.*   I'll go no more.
> I am afraid to think what I have done;
> Look on't again I dare not.

Lady Macbeth seizes the daggers and returns them herself. Left
alone, Macbeth gazes on his hands:

> What hands are here? Ha! they pluck out mine eyes.
> Will all great Neptune's ocean wash this blood
> Clean from my hand? No, this my hand will rather
> The multitudinous seas incarnadine,
> Making the green one red.

Macbeth's purgatory is in full function. Indeed, it started, as
we have seen, even before the actual commission of the crime.
But it is purgatory, not hell. Redemption follows repentance.
Macbeth's repentance—oh, such sincere repentance—begins im-
mediately after the crime. There is a loud knocking at the gate.
Lady Macbeth returns, and shows him her hands:

> My hands are of your color; but I shame
> To wear a heart so white. I hear a knocking
> At the south entry. Retire we to our chamber.
> A little water clears us of this deed;
> How easy is it then!

He does not move. She calls to him: "Your constancy hath left
you unattended. Hark! more knocking. Get on your nightgown,
lest occasion call us and show us to be watchers." He still does
not move. She shakes him: "Be not lost so poorly in your
thoughts!" The knocking continues. Finally there is wrung from
his heart a piteous supplication: "Wake Duncan with thy knocking. I would thou couldst!"

The knocking has awakened the drunken porter. The comic
scene that follows has evoked considerable controversy. It would
not be surprising if the objections to it came only from classically
conditioned people, like the French, for instance, to whom the

inclusion of comedy in a serious play introducing royalty is an artistic monstrosity. But lovers of Shakespeare have gone so far as to deny Shakespeare the authorship of the scene. The great romantic German poet and playwright, Friedrich Schiller, in his translation of the play, replaced the drunken porter with a sober porter singing a spring song. This failure of comprehension is amazing. It should not be difficult to understand that if this scene were omitted, the powerful discovery scene that follows would be presented to an audience emotionally exhausted by the ghastly murder scene. A relaxing interlude is imperative. But Shakespeare has a way of giving his apparently irrelevant interpolations a subtly significant relevancy. For example, in *Julius Caesar,* when Brutus and Cassius engage in a private conference, the other characters on the stage get interested in the question as to where on the horizon the sun would rise. Two opinions are advanced; then the surly Casca steps in:

> You shall confess that you are both deceiv'd.
> Here, *as I point my sword,* the sun arises,
> Which is a great way growing on the south,
> Weighing the youthful season of the year.
> Some two months hence up higher to the north
> He first presents his fire; and the high east
> Stands, as the Capitol, directly here.

And he points his sword significantly directly at the Capitol, where he intends to use that sword in a little while. The location of the Capitol had not been part of the discussion. So here in *Macbeth*: the porter is amusing himself playing the role of "porter of hell-gate." He is not at all aware of what a hell he is at that very moment actually porter.

The knocking at the gate is the knocking of Nemesis. The first man to enter Macbeth's stronghold after the murder is the man destined to avenge that murder—Macduff. He has an early appointment with the king. Macbeth directs him to Duncan's chamber. He returns at once and rouses up the house with his report. Macbeth pretends not to understand. "What is't you say?"

Macduff. Approach the chamber, and destroy your sight
With a new Gorgon. Do not bid me speak;
See, and then speak yourselves.

Macbeth runs up to the chamber. Lady Macbeth enters:

What's the business,
That such a hideous trumpet calls to parley
The sleepers of the house? Speak, speak!
　　Macduff.　　　　　　　　　　O gentle lady,
'Tis not for you to hear what I can speak;
The repetition in a woman's ear
Would murder as it fell.

He turns to Banquo, who just then enters:

　　　　　　　　　　　　　　O Banquo, Banquo,
Our Royal master's murder'd!

Now Lady Macbeth betrays her guilt in her first speech: "What, in our house?" Not Macduff, but Banquo, who has been harboring suspicions, answers her. He looks her squarely in the eyes, and says simply: "Too cruel anywhere."

Macbeth returns from the death chamber. He had declared: "I am afraid to think what I have done; look on it again I dare not." Now he had been compelled to look on it again. Never were more earnest words spoken than these:

> Had I but died an hour before this chance,
> I had liv'd a blessed time; for, from this instant,
> There's nothing serious in mortality.
> All is but toys; renown and grace is dead;
> The wine of life is drawn, and the mere lees
> Is left this vault to brag of.

Quite different is Macbeth's answer to Donaldbain, who asks: "What is amiss?"

> 　　　　　　　　　　You are, and do not know't.
> The spring, the head, the fountain of your blood
> Is stopp'd; the very source of it is stopp'd.

This artificial rhetoric only mystifies Donalbain, so Macduff explains bluntly: "Your royal father's murder'd." "O, by whom?" Lenox informs him: "Those of his chamber, as it seem'd, had done it." *As it seem'd*; Macbeth and his wife hear suspicion all around them; and when Macbeth comes out with, "O, I do repent me of my fury, that I did kill them," Macduff is electrified: "Wherefore did you so?" Macbeth proceeds to deliver himself of a flood of the same kind of artificial rhetoric which he had addressed to Donalbain. Lady Macbeth listens to her husband enmeshing himself more hopelessly with every word, and she can endure no more. At this critical moment, when Macbeth needs her support more than ever, she collapses, and is carried out. From now on, Macbeth's deeds lie upon his own head. To be sure, she rallies long enough to save the situation at the banquet when the ghost of Banquo appears to Macbeth, but she no longer influences his actions.

Banquo knows that under the circumstances not one of them can escape being suspected. He steps forward to proclaim his own innocence, and his willingness to join in ferreting out the guilty one:

> And when we have our naked frailties hid,
> That suffer in exposure, let us meet
> And question this most bloody piece of work,
> To know it further. Fear and scruples shake us.
> In the great hand of God I stand, and thence
> Against the undivulg'd pretence I fight
> Of treasonous malice.

Macbeth and his wife are crowned king and queen. The first words we hear from Macbeth's lips the first time we see him alone after the coronation are: "To be thus is nothing;" the first words from Lady Macbeth: "Nought's had, all's spent." This is the cold realization of the dream in which they had esteemed the possession of "the golden round" to be "the ornament of life." Macbeth does not feel safe. He is afraid of Banquo, who had taken no pains to conceal his attitude. He is bitterly envious of Banquo. He cannot forget the difference in the Weird Sisters' prophecies as they applied to him and to Banquo respectively:

>   ... prophet-like
> They hail'd him father to a line of kings.
> Upon my head they placed a fruitless crown,
> And put a barren sceptre in my gripe,
> Thence to be wrench'd with an unlineal hand,
> No son of mine succeeding. If it be so,
> For Banquo's issue have I fil'd my mind;
> For them the gracious Duncan have I murder'd;
> Put rancors in the vessel of my peace
> Only for them; and mine eternal jewel
> Given to the common enemy of man,
> To make them kings, the seed of Banquo kings!

> Rather than so, come fate into the list,
> And champion me to th'utterance!

He will fight with fate to the limit! This man is mad. Does he expect to come out victor in the end? He does not think so far ahead. He does not realize that his first murder started a chain reaction. Now it is Banquo's turn. He thinks that if he kills Banquo the rancors will depart from the vessel of his peace. With Banquo out of the way, he will think of Macduff; then, devil-driven, of another, and another, until Scotland will be a land "almost afraid to know itself . . . where sighs and groans and shrieks that rend the air are made, not mark'd."

Lady Macbeth will not show her own distress in the presence of her husband. Him she must comfort:

> How now, my lord! why do you keep alone,
> Of sorriest fancies your companions making,
> Using those thoughts which should indeed have died
> With them they think on? Things without remedy
> Should be without regard; what's done is done.

But for him what's done is not yet done. His fears at the outset now prove not to have been groundless. Then he felt that he would be less reluctant to commit the crime "if it were done when 'tis done," the first *done* meaning *finished*. It proved to be only the beginning:

> We have scorch'd the snake, not kill'd it;
> She'll close and be herself, whilst our poor malice
> Remains in danger of her former tooth.

He envies Duncan his peaceful slumber:

> Better be with the dead
> Whom we, to gain our peace, have sent to peace,
> Than on the torture of the mind to lie
> In restless ecstasy. Duncan is in his grave;
> After life's fitful fever he sleeps well.
> Treason has done his worst; nor steel, nor poison,
> Malice domestic, foreign levy, nothing,
> Can touch him further.

To his wife's continued efforts at comfort he can only say, "O, full of scorpions is my mind, dear wife." To rid his mind of those scorpions he hires murderers to do away with Banquo and his son Fleance. But the scorpions remain; for Fleance, through whom Banquo is to become "father to a line of kings," escapes. His defeat in the first round of his battle with fate only hardens his heart the more:

> For mine own good
> All causes shall give way. I am in blood
> Stepp'd in so far that, should I wade no more,
> Returning were as tedious as go o'er.

To Lady Macbeth such an insane determination argues mental fatigue: "You lack the season of all nature, sleep." With bitter mockery he replies: "Come, we'll to sleep." And we remember the loud call: "Sleep no more! Macbeth shall sleep no more!" This prophecy too has been fulfilled.

Macbeth, however, does not accept his wife's explanation. To his mind the reason for his distress is lack of experience. He has not yet become hardened to crime:

> My strange and self-abuse
> Is the initiate fear that wants hard use.
> We are yet but young in deed.

He says "we," but he will travel alone. His wife is a defeated woman. Having leapt to what she thought was the pinnacle of life, she discovers that "nought's had, all's spent." He does not need her stimulus any more. Already he has planned the murder of Banquo without her knowledge. Condescendingly he hints at it to her:

> Ere the bat hath flown
> His cloister'd flight, ere to black Hecate's summons
> The shard-borne beetle, with his drowsy hums,
> Hath rung night's yawning peal,
> There shall be done a deed of dreadful note.
> *Lady Macbeth.* What's to be done?
> *Macbeth.* Be innocent of the knowledge, dearest chuck,
> Till thou applaud the deed.

He plans to launch his further operations with a visit to the Weird Sisters:

> I will tomorrow,
> And betimes I will, to the weird sisters.
> More shall they speak; for now I am bent to know,
> By the worst means, the worst.

Perhaps there is an inconsistency here. At his first encounter with the Weird Sisters they are mysterious beings, both to him and to Banquo. The latter asks:

> What are these,
> So wither'd and so wild in their attire,
> That look not like th' inhabitants o' the earth,
> And yet are on't? Live you? or are you aught
> That men may question?

When Macbeth commands them: "Tell me more. Speak, I charge you," they ignore him and vanish into air. Now they have a local habitation. Macbeth knows where to find them, and he assumes that he has power to command them. When he arrives they are engaged in cooking a witch's brew. There is no attempt to endow them with any special dignity. The are just the ordinary broom-riding witches in whom Shakespeare's audience believed, and belief in whom marks a black page in American history. Indeed, belief in the existence of spirits of evil, embodied and unembodied, hovering among human beings, ready to do them harm, has never died out, and most people believe in it implicitly today. If anyone considers this a reckless statement, let him ask himself about it as he consults his horoscope.

Macbeth is "bent to know, by the worst means, the worst," the worst means being, of course, consultation with the witches, to Shakespeare's audience a heinous offense. It was trafficking with the devil. He wishes to know the worst. To be sure, he learns the worst, namely, that Banquo's issue shall reign in Scotland. Nevertheless, so far as the present is concerned, he is left confirmed in perfect security. The witches conjure up an Apparition, who proclaims:

> Be lion-mettled, proud, and take no care
> Who chafes, who frets, or where conspirers are.
> Macbeth shall never vanquish'd be, until
> Great Birnam wood to high Dunsinane hill
> Shall come against him.

Macbeth naturally concludes, "That will never be." Another Apparition warns him to "beware Macduff," but a third Apparition promptly calls to him:

Be bloody, bold, and resolute; laugh to scorn
The pow'r of man; for none of woman born

Shall harm Macbeth.
   Macbeth. Then live, Macduff: what need I fear of thee?
But yet I'll make assurance double sure
And take a bond of fate. Thou shalt not live;
That I may tell pale-hearted fear it lies,
And sleep in spite of thunder.

But Macduff has fled to England to raise an army against
Macbeth. When Macbeth hears of it he explodes:

> Fled to England!
> Time, thou anticipat'st my dread exploits:
> The flighty purpose never is o'ertook
> Unless the deed go with it. From this moment
> The very firstlings of my heart shall be
> The firstlings of my hand. And even now,
> To crown my thoughts with acts, be it thought and done.
> The castle of Macduff I will surprise;
> Seize upon Fife; give to the edge o'the sword
> His wife, his babes, and all unfortunate souls
> That trace him in his line.

He is as good as his word, sinking to the lowest level of depravity
a human being can reach.

Lady Macbeth has not been partner in her husband's steep
descent into savagery. She is a sick woman. She walks in her
sleep. The memory of a dark night oppresses her. She must have
a light by her always; even in her sleep-walking she carries it
with her. She sets it down only to rub her hands, which is an
accustomed action with her, for a quarter of an hour. She speaks
in her sleep:

Yet here's a spot. Out, damned spot! out, I say!—One, two: why, then
'tis time to do't.—Hell is murky!—Fie, my lord, fie! a soldier, and
afeard?—What need we fear who knows it, when none can call our
power to account?—Yet who would have thought the old man to have
so much blood in him? The thane of Fife had a wife: where is she
now?—What, will these hands ne'er be clean?—No more o' that, my
lord, no more o' that: you mar all with this starting. Here's the smell
of the blood still: all the perfumes of Arabia will not sweeten this
little hand. Oh! oh! oh!

Once it was: "A little water clears us of this deed: how easy is it
then?"

Macbeth consults the doctor: "How does your patient, doctor?

Doctor.   Not so sick, my lord,
As she is troubled with thick-coming fancies
That keep her from her rest.
Macbeth.   Cure her of that!
Canst thou not minister to a mind diseas'd,
Pluck from the memory a rooted sorrow,
Raze out the written troubles of the brain,
And with some sweet oblivious antidote
Cleanse the stuff'd bosom of that perilous stuff
Which weighs upon the heart?
Doctor.   Therein the patient
Must minister to himself.
Macbeth. Throw physic to the dogs; I'll none of it.

He can particularize his wife's symptoms so accurately because
they are his own. Sardonically he harps still further on the doctor's ignorance:

> If thou couldst, doctor, cast
> The water of my land, find her disease,
> And purge it to a sound and pristine health,
> I would applaud thee to the very echo,
> That should applaud again.
> What rhubarb, senna, or what purgative drug,
> Would scour these English hence?

It cannot be that he does not know that *he* is his land's disease.
No. He is glutted with his country's blood, and is at last sobering
up. He would like to see his land restored to a sound and pristine
health. But it is too late. The English army has already invaded,
and the doctor can supply him with no purgative drug that will
scour them hence. He is tired of life. He has awakened to the
tragic failure he has made of it. Yearningly he rehearses what
might have been:

> I have lived long enough. My way of life
> Is fallen into the sere, the yellow leaf;
> And that which should accompany old age,
> As honor, love, obedience, troops of friends,
> I must not look to have, but, in their stead,
> Curses, not loud, but deep, mouth-honor, breath,
> Which the poor heart would fain deny, and dare not.

An author is all-powerful; he can arbitrarily decree any punishment he chooses for the wrongdoers he creates. But if the

mirror he holds up to life reflects a true image, the punishment will not be arbitrary; it will be the punishment that stern reality would inflict. Shakespeare kills Macbeth in the end, but death to Macbeth is a relief. His punishment lies in living a life without value or meaning, still longing for what gives life value. Thus his punishment does not merely fit the crime; it was inherent in the crime. His crime was wilfully rejecting the validity of the social law and withdrawing from its jurisdiction; his punishment was existence outside the pale of organized society. For a human being life's values can be derived only from human society.

Macbeth has become utterly apathetic. He hears the cry of women:

> I have almost forgot the taste of fears.
> The time has been, my senses would have cool'd
> To hear a night-shriek, and my fell of hair
> Would at a dismal treatise rouse and stir
> As life were in 't. I have supp'd full with horrors;
> Direness, familiar to my slaughterous thoughts.

The truth of his last statement receives immediate exemplification. We have seen that he loved his wife dearly. Yet now, when the report is brought that his wife is dead, he remains unmoved. She would have died sometime anyway:

> There would have been a time for such a word.
> To-morrow, and to-morrow, and to-morrow
> Creeps in this petty pace from day to day
> To the last syllable of recorded time;
> And all our yesterdays have lighted fools
> The way to dusty death. Out, out, brief candle!
> Life's but a walking shadow, a poor player
> That struts and frets his hour upon the stage,
> And then is heard no more. It is a tale
> Told by an idiot, full of sound and fury,
> Signifying nothing.

Life has lost all meaning for him. Yet he has not lost his manly courage, which once made him defy even the fates:

> I'll fight till from my bones my flesh be hack'd.
> Give me mine armor . . .
> The cry is still, "They come." Our castle's strength
> Will laugh a siege to scorn; here let them lie

Till famine and the ague eat them up.
Were they not forc'd with those that should be ours,
We might have met them dareful, beard to beard,
And beat them backward home.

The invading army having reached Birnam Wood, each soldier
cuts off a branch to carry before him, in order to camouflage its
approach. A sentinel runs to report to Macbeth:

Macbeth. Thou com'st to use thy tongue; thy story quickly.
Messenger. Gracious my lord,
I should report that which I say I saw,
But know not how to do it.
Macbeth.   Well, say, sir.
Messenger. As I did stand my watch upon the hill,
I look'd toward Birnam, and anon, methought,
The wood began to move.
Macbeth.   Liar and slave!
Messenger. Let me endure your wrath if't be not so.
Within this three mile may you see it coming;
I say, a moving grove.
Macbeth.   If thou speak'st false,
Upon the next tree shalt thou hang alive,
Till famine cling thee: if thy speech be sooth,
I care not if thou dost for me as much.
I pull in resolution, and begin
To doubt th' equivocation of the fiend
That lies like truth. "Fear not, till Birnam wood
Do come to Dunsinane;" and now a wood
Comes to Dunsinane. Arm, arm, and out!
Ring the alarum-bell! Blow, wind! come, wrack!
At least we'll die with harness on our back.

Macbeth leaves the castle to meet the enemy "dareful, beard
to beard." He hears a voice thundering behind him: "Turn, hell-
hound, turn!" He turns around and finds himself face to face with
Macduff. He shrinks back, but not out of fear. He still has faith
in the prophecy that he is invincible before a man of woman
born:

Of all men else I have avoided thee.
But get thee back; my soul is too much charg'd
With blood of thine already.

"My soul is too much charg'd with blood of thine already." If
repentance is a saving grace, then Macbeth is not headed toward

eternal damnation. Where there is a spark of humanity the human being is ultimately incorruptible. The Devil has lost again. He was defeated in his onslaught on Job; he is defeated in his onslaught on Macbeth. His allurements have been weighed and measured, and found wanting. He will try again with Faust and will be defeated again. *"Ein guter Mensch in seinem dunklen Drange, Ist sich des rechten Weges wohl bewusset"* and Macbeth was a good man.

Macduff attacks the unwilling Macbeth, and in the furious contest Macbeth informs Macduff:

> Thou losest labor.
> As easy mayst thou the intrenchant air
> With thy keen sword impress, as make me bleed:
> Let fall thy blade on vulnerable crests;
> I bear a charmed life, which must not yield
> To one of woman born.
>   *Macduff.*   Despair thy charm;
> And let the angel whom thou still hast serv'd
> Tell thee, Macduff was from his mother's womb
> Untimely ripp'd.
>   *Macbeth.* Accursed be the tongue that tells me so,
> For it has cow'd my better part of man!
> And be these juggling fiends no more believ'd
> That palter with us in a double sense,
> And keep the word of promise to our ear,
> And break it to our hope. I'll not fight with thee.

Rather late now to decide not to believe these juggling fiends. It would have been better had he heeded Banquo's warning at the outset, about the ways of "the instruments of darkness." Macduff taunts him with cowardice and disgrace; so he makes a decision:

> Though Birnam wood be come to Dunsinane,
> And thou oppos'd, being of no woman born,
> Yet I will try the last. Lay on, Macduff,
> And damn'd be him that first cries, "Hold, enough!"

Thus he dies fighting a hopeless battle like a hero. There is rejoicing in the land, and rightly so. But there is pity in our hearts. "I say unto you, that likewise joy shall be in heaven over one sinner that repenteth, more than ninety and nine just persons which need no repentance."

CHAPTER 5

Shakespeare and the Jew:
The Merchant of Venice

"**F**OR IT IS NOT one foe only that has risen up against us, but in every generation there have arisen those against us who sought to annihilate us." Once every year, for two thousand years, the head of the Jewish household has repeated this reminder, as part of the Passover Eve ritual commemorating the Exodus from Egypt. It sums up in brief the story of the Jewish people from Haman to Hitler. We shall go astray in our interpretation of human conduct if we do not bear in mind that the unremitting persecution of the Jew during Christian centuries has been practiced in a spirit of righteousness. In the fourth Gospel the Jew is coupled with the Devil as the condemned of the Almighty. Hence both were to be equally the objects of abhorrence. The persistent association of the two tended toward identification. In his book, *The Devil and the Jews*, Joshua Trachtenberg makes the point that the identification of the Jew with the Devil used to convey a much more literal connotation than it does today. When Launcelot Gobbo, in *The Merchant of Venice*, says "the Jew is the very devil incarnal," he is not indulging in an outright metaphor. Even today there are those in peasant cultures who, upon knowingly meeting a Jew for the first time, are puzzled by the absence of the horns.

Seeking to destroy the Jews has often been thus an act of virtue. Massacring the Jewish communities in the line of march of the Crusaders was a bid for Divine favor. When the saintly Godfrey of Bouillon, leader of the First Crusade, succeeded in taking the Holy City, he, by way of thanksgiving to the Lord, invited the Jews of Jerusalem into the synagogue—and set fire to the synagogue.

Jew-hatred received a fresh impetus in northern Europe at the coming of the Reformation, effected by the savage virulence of Martin Luther's onslaught against the Jews. To describe the

Jewish heart he coined a monstrous epithet: *Stocksteineisenteu-felhart* (stockstoneirondevilhard). One recalls Antonio's declaration in *The Merchant of Venice,* ending with:

> You may as well do any thing most hard,
> As seek to soften that—than which what's harder?—
> His Jewish heart.

He lauded the rulers who banished the Jews from their domains, and recommended total extermination. These facts of history must be borne in mind if we are to conceive the receptivity of the public for whom Shakespeare wrote *The Merchant of Venice.* Just how that public felt about the Jew is revealed in Falstaff's asserveration: "I am a Jew else, an Ebrew Jew."

Did Shakespeare class himself with that public? Was it not rather his impatience with that public that made him exclaim:

> Sure, He that made us with such large discourse,
> Looking before and after, gave us not
> That capability and god-like reason
> To fust in us unus'd.

Shakepeare was not a conformist. He had a contempt for those who traveled safely on the broad highway of public opinion. What withering scorn in Prince Hal's words addressed to Poins! "Thou art a blessed fellow to think as every man thinks. Never a man's thought in the world keeps the road-way better than thine." When the Burmese representative at the United Nations was asked in a television broadcast what impressed her first upon arriving in America, her prompt reply was: "The peculiar slant of your eyes." This was a complacency-shattering moment. Shakespeare would not have been stunned for a second, as the interviewer and the viewers were. He could put himself in the place of another and see the world through his eyes. The black suitor for the hand of Portia in *The Merchant of Venice* is proud of his color: "I would not change this hue." To him it is "the shadow'd livery of the burnish'd sun." The blackamoor Aaron in *Titus Andronicus* declares that black is superior to white. The black Othello is the most sympathetically treated of all Shakespeare's characters.

We point out that he was far ahead of his time. He repudiated the caste system. Perdita the shepherdess declares:

> I was not much afeard; for once or twice
> I was about to speak and tell him [the king] plainly,
> The selfsame sun that shines upon his court
> Hides not his visage from our cottage, but
> Look on alike.

He is deeply moved by the callous injustice inflicted on the masses. The pampered King Lear ennobled by suffering reaches the height of his regeneration in the realization of it. His memorable utterance on the subject is quoted on page (4).

A man of such breadth of vision will not be subject to the limitations that confine the mental horizon of ordinary men. His conception of man's potentiality expressed above in the quotation from *Hamlet* is further elaborated:

> What a piece of work is a man! How noble in reason! How infinite in faculty! . . . In apprehension how like a god!

This description we may, and we do, apply to Shakespeare himself. Such a man will not be swayed by the prejudices that control other men. Exhibition of anti-Semitism in other writers—a Dickens, a Thackeray—we may find disturbing, but we explain it on historic grounds. Shakespeare, however, we set apart from other writers. Can we accept the notion that this universal genius would acquiesce in the popular attitude toward the Jew that prevailed in his time? Many point to Shylock as proof that he did. Only through a careful scrutiny of the text of *The Merchant of Venice* and a realization of the conditions and circumstances that surrounded the creation and production of the play, can we hope to arrive at a satisfactory answer to the question.

How did Shakespeare come to write the play? Shakespeare was a member of a cooperative company for which he wrote his plays. The company paid for the play and it became its property, the author having no further control over it as an individual. The company, of course, was interested in a play that was calculated to make a hit. The theme of the cruel Jew had proved successful on the London stage at least twice before. Now whether the company suggested the subject or he determined on it himself, Shakespeare saw in it an opportunity to delight the London theater-goer and, at the same time, as I believe will become apparent as we go along, release something that was deep down in him.

The story of the play he wrote may be briefly summarized thus: The hard-hearted Jewish moneylender, Shylock, on the pretense of a merry joke, tricks the generous and noble-minded merchant, Antonio, into signing a bond in which the latter agrees, if he fails to return the three thousand ducats he was borrowing within three months, to forfeit a pound of flesh, to be cut off from the body nearest the heart. The merchant feels safe in signing, inasmuch as all his numerous ships laden with rich cargo were due in port long before the end of the three-month period. But, of course, the unexpected happens. All his ships, in different parts of the ocean are wrecked and he is called upon to pay the forfeit. The villain, however, is foiled in court at the last moment by Portia, a bright girl disguised as a lawyer, who points out that the bond allows him a pound of flesh only, but not a drop of blood, and only an exact pound—no more, no less. The impossibility of the terms is immediately manifest, and there is great rejoicing. This is the story to which Shakespeare's audience thrilled. This is what they wanted, and this is what he gave them.

But there may be more than one way of telling a story. Browning, for instance, in *The Ring and the Book,* tells a story, the same story, in ten different ways, depending on different points of view. Another way of telling the story of *The Merchant of Venice,* equally authentically by the text of the play, is as follows: Shylock is a money-lender, scrupulously honest in his dealings. ("Thrift is a blessing," he avers, "if men steal it not.") He is proud of his Jewish heritage, loves his daughter, fondly cherishes the memory of his wife, has a good word for his servant, views life with the high seriousness characteristic of his race, abominates the institution of slavery. Because he is a Jew he is subjected to vulgar indignities, particularly at the hands of the merchant Antonio, who makes a practice of kicking him and spitting in his face and humiliating him in crowds. This contumely Shylock endures with dignified resignation, aware that such is the inescapable lot of his people. It happens that this Antonio is compelled to come to Shylock for a loan. Shylock hopes that here is an opportunity to do something to mitigate Antonio's hostility. He offers to grant him the loan without interest. However, to make the transaction a formal one, he suggests, as "a merry sport," that if the money is not repaid within three months, Antonio shall forfeit a pound of flesh. Antonio agrees, for it is

clear that his commercial situation is so secure that the exaction
of the forfeiture is not even a remote possibility.

Shortly after this transaction one of Antonio's intimate friends,
Lorenzo, elopes with Shylock's daughter, Jessica, who takes with
her a substantial portion of her father's wealth. Shylock is heart-
broken. Then the impossible happens: all of Antonio's ships are
reported lost and Antonio is bankrupt. This is another blow for
Shylock. It means the additional loss of three thousand ducats.
In his distress he recalls the terms of the loan. Here was an unexpected opportunity to take revenge for all the torment inflicted
upon him, and he grimly determines to take advantage of it.

This story, too, Shakespeare tells his audience, but this story
did not register. More remarkable is the fact that it hardly regis-
ters, not only in the modern theater, where the speed of the
action prevents minute consideration of details, but even with
the modern reader, for whom the play unfolds in a more leisurely
fashion, so successful was Shakespeare in obscuring what would
have displeased his audience. How did he manage to do it? His
technique is really very simple. The effect of any passage calculated, taken by itself, to arouse sympathy with Shylock, is immediately nullified by the context.

When Shylock cites the Bible in justification of his profession
Antonio's comment is:

> The devil can cite Scripture for his purpose.
> An evil soul, producing holy witness,
> Is like a villain with a smiling cheek,
> A goodly apple rotten at the heart.
> O, what a goodly outside falsehood hath!

and any misgiving on the part of the audience is thus promptly
allayed. Shylock's comment on his servant Launcelot, "The patch
is kind enough," is continued with, "but a huge feeder." The
fatherly affection implicit in the expression, "Jessica my girl," is
lost on the spectator, whose attention is absorbed in the impending elopement, and the heartrending cry, "My daughter, O my
daughter," becomes ludicrous when coupled with "O my ducats."
A speech like the following would normally be calculated to
arouse sympathy:

> I am bid forth to supper, Jessica;
> There are my keys. But wherefore should I go?
> I am not bid for love; they flatter me.

But the next line reads:

> But yet I'll go in hate, to feed upon
> The prodigal Christian.

Shylock is oppressed by a premonition: "I am right loth to go.
There's some ill abrewing toward my rest," and the following
line brings a laugh: "For I did dream of moneybags tonight."
When he is informed that Jessica has exchanged a ring for a
monkey, his reaction is: "Thou torturest me, Tubal; it was my
turquoise; I had it of Leah when I was a bachelor." Surely here
is a moment when Shylock deserves sympathy, and the sentiment
expressed in the next line should intensify that sympathy. But the
grotesque image it conjures up brings a laugh even in the modern
theater: "I would not have given it for a wilderness of monkeys."

There are two passages, however, that cannot be so easily explained. These must be quoted in full. Shylock speaks:

> Signior Antonio, many a time and oft
> In the Rialto you have rated me
> About my moneys and my usances:
> Still have I borne it with a patient shrug,
> For sufferance is the badge of all our tribe.
> You call me misbeliever, cut-throat dog,
> And spit upon my Jewish gaberdine,
> And all for use of that which is mine own.
> Well then, it now appears you need my help:
> Go to, then; you come to me and you say,
> "Shylock, we would have moneys;" you say so,
> You, that did void your rheum upon my beard
> And foot me as you spurn a stranger cur
> Over your threshold: moneys is your suit.
> What should I say to you? Should I not say,
> "Hath a dog money? Is it possible
> A cur can lend three thousand ducats?" Or,
> Shall I bend low, and in a bondsman's key,
> With bated breath and whispering humbleness,
> Say this:—
> "Fair sir, you spat on me on Wednesday last;
> You spurn'd me such a day; another time
> You call'd me dog; and for these courtesies
> I'll lend you thus much moneys"?

Antonio's response is:

> I am as like to call thee so again,
> To spit on thee again, to spurn thee too.

This from the man who is presented as the noblest character in the play. His friends cannot find words to express his goodness. The other passage is even more striking:

He hath disgraced me, and hindered me half a million; laughed at my losses, mocked at my gains, scorned my nation, thwarted my bargains, cooled my friends, heated mine enemies; and what's his reason? I am a Jew. Hath not a Jew eyes? hath not a Jew hands, organs, dimensions, affections, passions? fed with the same food, hurt with the same weapons, subject to the same diseases, heated by the same means, warmed and cooled by the same winter and summer, as a Christian is? If you prick us do we not bleed? if you tickle us do we not laugh? If you poison us do we not die? and if you wrong us, shall live not revenge? If we are like you in the rest, we will resemble you in that. If a Jew wrong a Christian, what is his humility? Revenge. If a Christian wrong a Jew, what should his sufferance be by Christian example? Why, revenge. The villainy you teach me I will execute, and it shall go hard but I will better the instruction.

When Falstaff asseverates, as a consummation devoutly *not* to be wished, "I am a Jew else, an Ebrew Jew!" we know that it is Falstaff speaking; that it is just what Falstaff would say. There is no implication, one way or the other, of how Shakespeare himself felt. But who will venture the opinion that in having Shylock give utterance to this detailed catalogue Shakespeare was speaking in mockery? Indeed, if these two passages were all that was extant, would we not conclude that the lost play must have been an arraignment of the world's inhumanity toward the Jew? The utterances are direct and explicit, with no attempt this time at obscuration or offsetting—unless it be the final words of Shylock, in which he promises to better the instruction. How, then, did he dare present them before a Jew-hating audience? Was he not afraid of a riot? It will be easier for us to perceive the explanation if we realize that in certain parts of our country the advocacy of Blacks' equality *does* create riotous situations. Even in this day of computers and moon-rockets, the very President of the United States is an ally of men whose view of the Negro finds its root in the cruel mentality of the slaveowner. Just as absurd, even more so, would be a Jew's claim to equality in Shakespeare's day, for the Jew was not merely an inferior being; he was, as pointed out, of the kinship of the Devil. Shylock's exhortation does not even rate a reply. The matter is set right in the minds of the audience with Salanio's remark: "Here comes another of the tribe; another cannot be matched unless the Devil himself turn Jew."

Note particularly the lines,

> Still have I borne it with a patient shrug,
> For sufferance is the badge of all our tribe.

They are lines whose significance only dawns on one gradually. Where did Shakespeare have an opportunity to observe the behavior of Jews, and where did he learn of an interpretation of history from the Jewish point of view? His world regarded what the Jew had to endure, not as suffering, but as punishment, the infliction of which was a virtuous Christian act. There were few Jews in London with whom he could have discussed the question. What books were available to him? Some believe that he visited Venice. If he did, and made it a point to associate with Jews in the Ghetto in order to penetrate their souls and learn their history as *they* knew it, that alone would prove what an extraordinarily broad-minded genius he was. But there is no evidence that he was ever out of England. That he achieved such understanding nevertheless, demonstrates that he was that kind of genius. In this connection, his known interest in the writings of the half-Jew Montaigne, who preached tolerance, has significance.

The accuracy of one detail in the second version of the story of the play is bound to be questioned, namely, that Shylock did not think of exacting the forfeiture of the pound of flesh at the time of the contract, but decided on that procedure only after the Christians had stolen his daughter. Shakespeare is careful to emphasize and reemphasize that Antonio's financial situation is perfectly secure:

> I thank my fortune for it,
> My ventures are not in one bottom trusted,
> Nor in one place; nor is my whole estate
> Upon the fortune of this present year.

And again:

> In this there can be no dismay;
> My ships come home a month before the day.

And in fact all his ships do come home; without the rumor that all his ships were lost there would have been no play. Antonio's declaration that his whole estate is not trusted "upon the fortune of this present year," so that even if all his ships go down he will still be financially secure, is overlooked even as it is spoken. Shylock was no fool. He knew what to count on and what not to count on, and the loan of three thousand ducats without interest would be a profitable investment if it mitigated Antonio's active enmity. But Shakespeare wants his audience to regard Shylock's proposal as a deliberate trick, and so create suspense. The nature of the penalty is sufficient for that; but he makes assurance doubly sure by having Shylock say to himself a little earlier: "If I can catch him once upon the hip, I will feed fat the ancient grudge I bear him." Gratiano taunts Shylock with these words in the trial scene. By this time the audience has forgotten that nobody heard Shylock mutter them. The spectator has no time to consider that Shylock has no jurisdiction over the storms at sea. To him the bond is the opportunity Shylock has been seeking to catch Antonio upon the hip. But the play supplies proof that Shylock did not give the condition expressed in the bond another thought. Does he think of it when he hears of Antonio's bankruptcy? Not at all:

Salarino. But tell us, do you hear whether Antonio have any loss at sea or no?

Shylock. There I have another bad match.

To him Antonio's bankruptcy was another bad match, another misfortune piled on. It meant the loss of an additional three thousand ducats. If you want to know what is on a man's mind catch him off guard. It is only as he proceeds that it dawns upon him that here was an opportunity for revenge. Nor is this all. Within a moment he has, in his anguish, forgotten about it. When he meets Tubal he has to be reminded of it:

Shylock. The curse never fell upon our nation till now; I never felt it till now . . . and no satisfaction, no revenge; nor no ill luck stirring but what lights on my shoulders; no sighs but of my breathing; no tears but of my shedding.

Tubal. Yes, other men have ill luck too. Antonio, as I heard in Genoa,—

Shylock. What, what, what? ill luck? ill luck?

It is clear, then, that the pound-of-flesh clause in the bond was not a deliberately planned trick to catch Antonio upon the hip.

For the sake of a fair estimate of Shakespeare's treatment of Shylock attention must be called to two facts. One is that the story of the pound of flesh was not invented by Shakespeare. It is an old story, and originally did not involve a Jew. Making the villain a Jew was a later refinement. The other, and more important, fact is that *The Merchant of Venice* is not primarily concerned with Shylock; it is primarily concerned with the romantic love affair of Portia and Bassanio. Bassanio needs money to court Portia effectively, and Shylock provides that money. In this way he is brought into the story. He is the chief figure in the sub-plot, and disappears before the end of the fourth act, when the sub-plot is terminated. This fact comes as a surprise to many, and readers are further surprised to discover, as they turn the leaves, how few are the appearances of Shylock in the play. Yet Shylock is the character we are most interested in, and—the character in whom Shakespeare too was most interested. The result is that the play is thrown out of kilter. It is disabled both in structure and in characterization. The closing act is a lovely moonlight idyl, but a perfunctory, almost irrelevant, answer to the conventional requirement of a fifth act. To give it any substance Shakespeare had to devise the ring episode at the end of Act IV. The main plot realy terminates in the third act, when Bassanio picks the right casket. Nobody feels that the consummation of the marriage could be permanently frustrated by the unhappy plight of Antonio. Indeed, the fifth act is frequently dropped in performance to give Shylock greater proportional prominence. He alone looms large in the play. It is his role that the leading actor assumes. Bassanio, the protagonist in the main plot, shrinks into insignificance beside him. He does not at all approach the standard an audience envisions in the hero lover worthy of success in his courtship. He is a light-headed young man, who repeatedly borrows money without returning it. He is a fourflusher, a fortune hunter who borrows money to put on a big front before the wealthy girl he is about to woo. His character is revealed, as is customary in Shakespeare, in the first speech he utters when he enters the scene: "Good signiors both, when shall we laugh? Say when?" Yet this is the man selected to be the object of the noble Portia's affection:

> *Nerissa.* Do you not remember, lady, in your father's time, a Venetian, a scholar and a soldier, that came hither in the company of the Marquis of Montferrat?
> *Portia.* Yes, yes; it was Bassanio.
> *Nerissa.* True, madam; he of all the men that my foolish eyes looked upon, was the best deserving a fair lady.
> *Portia.* I remember him well, and I remember him worthy of thy praise.

What inconsistency! This does not at all describe the Bassanio we have been introduced to. Furthermore, the words that issue from Bassanio's mouth in the casket scene represent mature wisdom that could be achieved by one who has viewed life seriously, and has meditated long upon it. Such a man was certainly not Bassanio. After Bassanio makes the correct choice Portia thus addresses him:

> The full sum of me
> Is sum of nothing; which, to term in gross,
> Is an unlesson'd girl, unschool'd, unpractis'd;
> Happy in this, she is not yet so old
> But she can learn; happier in this,
> She is not bred so dull but she can learn;
> Happiest of all is that her gentle spirit
> Commits itself to yours to be directed,
> As from her lord, her governor, her king.

This is almost intolerable. The noble-minded and brilliant Portia to learn from, and be directed by, the gay adventurer Bassanio! Thus we have one Bassanio in relation to Portia, another in relation to the rest of the play. It cannot be maintained that Shakespeare was unaware of this inconsistency. He was forced into it by his interest in Shylock. The latter must be made to tower above his environment. Bassanio's companions are as frivolous as he. Goethe pointed out that Rosencrantz and Guildenstern in *Hamlet* are not differentiated because they are supposed to represent a multiplicity of courtiers—all alike. Similarly, aside from Antonio and Gratiano, Shakespeare does not attempt to differentiate between the friends of Bassanio. They represent the light-hearted and light-headed youth of Venice. He hardly attempts to differentiate between their names: Salanio, Salario, Salerio. Gratiano is as gay as the rest, but he also has some common sense, which is not appreciated by his fellows. He reads Antonio a sensible and timely lecture, and Antonio's comment is: "Is that anything now?" and Bassanio adds: "Gratiano speaks an infinite deal of nothing, more than any man in Venice." This is the milieu in which Shylock moves in scornful isolation:

Gratiano. Can no prayers pierce thee?
Shylock. No, none that thou hast wit enough to make....
Thou but offend'st thy lungs to speak so loud:
Repair thy wit, good youth, or it will fall
To cureless ruin.

In contrast with the levity which surrounds him Shylock maintains a dignified seriousness. When he hears that a masquerade would be passing before his door he exclaims:

"What! are there masques? Hear you me, Jessica;
Lock up my doors; and when you hear the drum,
And the vile squeaking of the wry-neck'd fife,
Clamber not you up to the casements then,
Nor thrust your head into the public street
To gaze on Christian fools with varnish'd faces,
But stop my house's ears; I mean my casements.
Let not the sound of shallow foppery enter
My sober house.

Note the loftiness of sentiment and diction. "Let not the sound of shallow foppery enter my sober house." The words might have been uttered by one of the Hebrew prophets.[1] But in the minds of the theater-goers of those days the sentiment expressed by Shylock was associated with the Puritans, therefore to be despised. But not in Shakespeare's opinion. In Shakespeare's fellow dramatists the Puritan is a frequent butt of humor and satire.

---

[1] Shakespeare did not know Jewish life at first hand (otherwise he would not have had Shylock eat at Bassanio's house, or cite the New Testament) yet it is extraordinary how truly he comprehended the Jewish spirit. That spirit was placed in historical perspective by Dr. S. Baeck in *Commentary*, February, 1949: "It was a struggle to decide whether the gaze should be directed towards Egypt and Babylonia or towards Mount Sinai ... In Israel the Prophets were victorious in the end, and thereby the Jewish spirit, and with it the Jewish people, was preserved."

But not in Shakespeare. Evidently he saw in Puritanism something to be respected. In *Twelfth Night* he has one revealing comment. When Malvolio is accused of being a Puritan, the response is: "The devil a Puritan that he is, or any thing constantly, but a time-pleaser." Here again Shakespeare reveals his unusual breadth of mind.

It is also significant that the attack on the institution of slavery is put into the mouth of Shylock, a Jew:

> You have among you many a purchased slave,
> Which, like your asses and your dogs and mules,
> You use in abject and in slavish parts,
> Because you bought them. Shall I say to you,
> Let them be free, marry them to your heirs?
> Why sweat they under burdens? Let their beds
> Be made as soft as yours, and let their palates
> Be season'd with such viands.

To how many of Shakespeare's contemporaries would such a thought have occurred? Indeed, it was a daring thing on Shakespeare's part to give expression to it, in an age when Queen Elizabeth herself engaged in the slave trade in partnership with Drake and Hawkins. Example after example emphasizes Shakespeare's breadth of vision.

Too much has been made of the fact that Shylock is defeated by a legal quibble. We may resent it, and Shakespeare probably smiled at the childishness of it; but what a thrilling moment it provided for the audience! And Shakespeare wrote the play for that audience, not for us. To evaluate the play as a theater production, we must put ourselves in the place of that audience. The way the court scene is built up to a climax is a masterpiece of dramatic suspense. Yet right through it runs a thread of bitter irony. At the beginning the duke exhorts Shylock to be merciful to Antonio; "We all expect a gentle answer, Jew." The gentle answer that Shylock could expect from that same Antonio was, "I am as like to spit on thee again, to spurn thee too." Then Portia grandly lectures Shylock on the quality of mercy. What mercy had ever been shown him? Kick him, spurn him like a cur, void your rheum upon his beard, earnestly promise to do it again—then treat him to a solemn sermon on the beneficence of mercy. Will anyone maintain that Shakespeare was so naive as not to perceive the irony in this situation? The absence of dignified regularity in the conduct of the trial is pointed up by Shakespeare when he makes the duke, after he has pronounced sentence, declare that if Shylock does not agree to the new condition suggested by Antonio, he will retract the pardon he has just granted. But all this escapes the audience. The greater the pressure upon Shylock the greater its delight.

Except for a bawdy speech by the irrepressible Gratiano, Shakespeare brings the play to a close with a significant reminder of the irresponsible levity that characterized the group arrayed against Shylock:

Portia.   How now, Lorenzo!
My clerk hath some good comforts too for you.
Nerissa. Ay, and I'll give them him without a fee.
There do I give to you and Jessica,
From the rich Jew, a special deed of gift,
After his death, of all he dies possess'd of.
Lorenzo., you drop manna in the way
Of starved people.

"Starved people." Already the wealth stolen from Shylock has been squandered—an eventuality for which Shakespeare prepared us when he let us know that the eloping couple had spent four score ducats in one night, and that the unfeeling Jessica had disposed of a precious ring, doubly precious because it was a gift from her mother to her father during their courtship, for a monkey. Her father "would not have given it for a wilderness of monkeys."

If, then, Shakespeare's aim was, as it had to be, to write a play that would succeed in the theater, why did he weave into it so much that, if more evident, would not only have assured its failure, but not impossibly have jeopardized his own safety? He surely did not anticipate that in some future and more enlightened age people would read his play with open eyes and learn how he himself felt. It was not customary in those days for playwrights to think of posterity. The explanation is that a great artist not only addresses a public, but also gives expression to his own deep self. To have drawn Shylock as the Elizabethan audience would have wanted him to (and as he succeeded in making it believe that he had) would have done violence to his own artistic and intellectual integrity. Perhaps, too, we have here an instance which illustrates "that inexplicable element of every highest poetical nature which causes it to cover up its real purpose and meanings", affirmed by Walt Whitman.

It must be remembered, in justice to Shakespeare, that in presenting a play that gave the audience an opportunity to indulge its anti-Jewish animus, he knew that he was not imperiling the welfare of any Jewish community; for there was no Jewish community in England on which a mob might vent its fury. Not tenable is the prevailing idea that the play was written to take advantage of the anti-Jewish fever raging in London as a result of the hanging after a long-drawn-out trial of Doctor Roderigo Lopez, the Queen's Jewish physician, accused by his enemy Essex of complicity in a plot to poison Elizabeth. That hanging had taken place three years back. No popular fever can rage that long. Nevertheless, one cannot doubt that the senseless fury of the population at the time spurred his attention to the Jew and his history, and planted thoughts in him that matured in the course of those three years.

In his treatment of Shylock, perhaps more than in anything else, Shakespeare reveals "how noble in reason, how infinite in faculties, in apprenhension how like a god" he was.

Naturally, the character of Shylock has had a powerful attraction for talented actors, and we have been treated to some good performances. Perhaps the better, the worse. A swastika painted on a synagogue wall might conceivably be an admirable piece of workmanship. To what extent does the audience faced by the modern actor differ materially from that for which Shakespeare wrote? I recently had the opportunity to witness a university performance of *The Merchane of Venice*. The response of the student audience painfully recalled a presentation of the Oberammergau Passion Play at which I was present in 1910. The image that has remained most vividly painted in my memory is that of the women wringing their hands and muttering *"Die verfluchten Juden, die verfluchten Juden."* We are told that *The Merchant of Venice* was Hitler's favorite play. The attempts of some actors in our day to let a more or less sympathetic Shylock emerge have failed. Inevitably. Mr. Michael Langham, the distinguished director of the Stratford, Ontario, Shakespeare Festival, declares: "Shakespeare at his greatest, with all his stops out, remains, in my view, always the subtlest of writers. Frankly, I have never seen (I have certainly never directed) a performance of a Shakespearean tragedy which even began to match the stupendous aspirations of the text." How, then, can we expect a director to reveal what Shakespeare took pains to conceal.

Just how far ahead of his time—or should we say our time—was William Shakespeare? Who will venture to say? During World War II a Bible was distributed among our soldiers, containing a footnote reading: "The Jews are the synagogue of Satan." When the editor was asked why he had inserted that uncalled-for footnote, his reply was simple and direct: "Because it's the truth."

The American Nazi Party has, as an organization, all but disappeared. But in the 1968 Presidential elections we witnessed a Third Party candidate electrify a nation and intimidate candidates in both major parties with his primitive, fascist-like appeal. We in the United States still elect Governors who stand on staunchly segregationist platforms. There are still stones thrown through synagogue windows (tossed, no doubt, with the hope that the "devil" will be given a good knock in the head). Still, the small town notion exists that "outside-agitator" equals "Jew." Still there are quotas, invisible barriers, restricted clubs. And today, in our universities, while man is in the process of conquering space, it has become appallingly enough, fashionable once again to link differences in racial background with the inherent ability to intellectually achieve.

How far ahead *was* Shakespeare?

Index

(*The works of Shakespeare are listed under his name*)

125